Classroom PATTERNS
for Children's Ministry

STANDARD PUBLISHING

Cincinnati, Ohio

Classroom Patterns for Children's Ministry

The Standard Publishing Company, Cincinnati, Ohio
A division of Standex International Corporation

Credits

Cover design: Sandi Welch
Inside illustrations: Daniel A. Grossmann
Project editor: Christine Spence
Acquisitions editor: Ruth Frederick

06 05 04 03 02 01 00 99   5 4 3 2 1

ISBN   0-7847-0975-0

Contents

How to Reproduce Patterns

PHOTOCOPY

The quickest way to reproduce patterns is by photocopying. This book is designed for easy photocopying. There are no patterns within other patterns, and several different sizes of some objects are provided to avoid the need to enlarge or reduce. Quick Copy Tip: If you need many copies of one object, photocopy the object several times. Then cut and tape the copies to one piece of paper, so you can photocopy several objects at one time.

GRID

1. Divide the original pattern into one-inch squares.
2. Divide a larger piece of paper into two-inch, three-inch, or four-inch squares, depending on how much you want to enlarge the pattern.
3. Copy the original pattern square by square onto a larger sheet.

TISSUE PAPER

1. Place a piece of tissue paper over the desired pattern.
2. Trace the pattern onto the tissue paper with a pencil.
3. Place the tissue paper on the paper for the pattern, and trace over the penciled pattern with a felt-tip marker. The marker will bleed through the tissue paper and the pattern will be printed on the construction paper.

OVERHEAD PROJECTOR

1. Trace the pattern onto a clear transparency.
2. Project the pattern onto paper or poster board using an overhead projector.
3. Adjust the size of the patterns by moving the projector closer to or farther from the paper.
4. Trace, cut out, and color the patterns you want to use.

Happy-sad stickers

WHAT YOU NEED
Face patterns from pages 49-51
White glue
Vinegar
Peppermint extract
Paint brushes
Markers

WHAT YOU DO

1 Reduce and photocopy the face patterns from pages 49-51. Make a whole page of sticker-size faces for each child.

2 Make a solution of 2 parts white glue, 1 part vinegar, and a few drops of peppermint extract.

3 Allow children to color the faces with markers. Then show them how to paint a light coating of the glue solution on the backs of their sticker pages. Allow the pages to dry. Children can cut out and moisten the face stickers to attach them.

* Encourage children to give stickers to a friend and tell them about Jesus.
* Tell children to add a sticker to their school notebook every time they choose to do right.

stencils

WHAT YOU NEED

Simple patterns, such as the heart (page 117), star (page 81), butterfly (page 9),
　　leaf (page 35), or flower (page 36)
Card board or heavy plastic for making stencils
Scissors or X-acto knife
Art paper
Tempera paint
Paint brushes

WHAT YOU DO

1 Trace and cut the individual stencil patterns from poster board or plastic.

2 Let children choose a stencil pattern, lay it on the paper, and paint over it.

* Make a thank-you picture to God for things he made.
* Stencil the star the wise men followed to find Jesus. Sprinkle with glitter.
* Cover your classroom door with paper. Allow children to stencil autumn leaves
for a seasonal door decoration.
* For older children, use latex paint and stencil brushes. Guide them to choose the
patterns and stencil designs on the walls of your classroom.

Bible Paper Doll

WHAT YOU NEED

Bible figure, clothing, and accessory patterns from pages 60-62
Poster board
Heavy paper
Scissors
Markers
Re-sticking tape
Glue

WHAT YOU DO

1 Cut the Bible figure pattern from poster board or lightweight cardboard. Copy and cut the clothing and accessories from heavyweight paper and color them or allow the children to color.

2 Glue a piece of re-sticking tape, sticky side up, in the center of the Bible figure. Glue pieces of re-sticking tape to the backs of the clothing and accessories.

3 Put the clothing and accessories together to make different Bible figures.

* Use the figure as you tell the story of David. Make David the shepherd boy, with a staff and simple clothing. Then make David the king, with a crown and royal clothing.
* Allow children to make their own Bible figures and use them to tell each other Bible stories.

Borders

The following pages contain border patterns for you to use with your bulletin boards and displays. Use the following instructions to make your borders.

1. Decide on the width you want the border to be. Enlarge or reduce your border pattern to this size. See the instructions on page 4.

2. Cut strips of paper into this width.

3. Fold strips of paper, so that you end up with the right size for the pattern. All the patterns are square. For example, if your pattern is two inches in width, cut paper 2" x 12" and fold into six equal pieces.

4. Lay the pattern so sides touch folds and draw around it.

5. Cut out the pattern making sure that you do not cut on the folds.

6. Make enough border strips to go around the edge of your board or display.

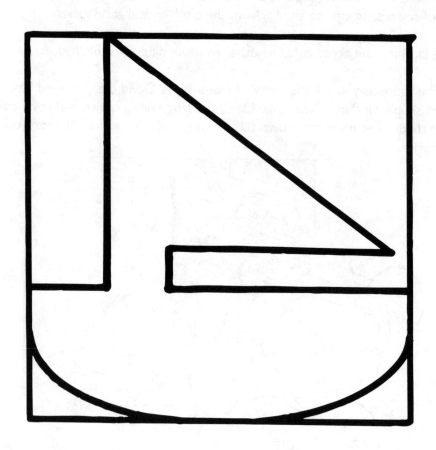

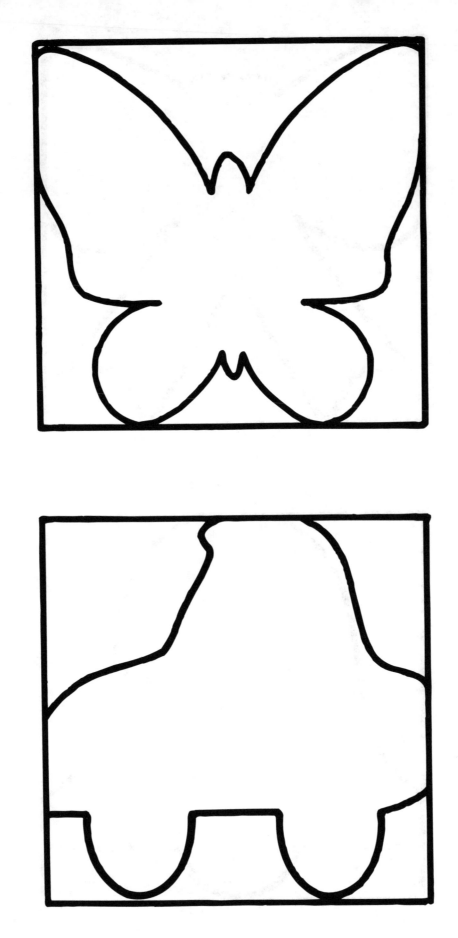

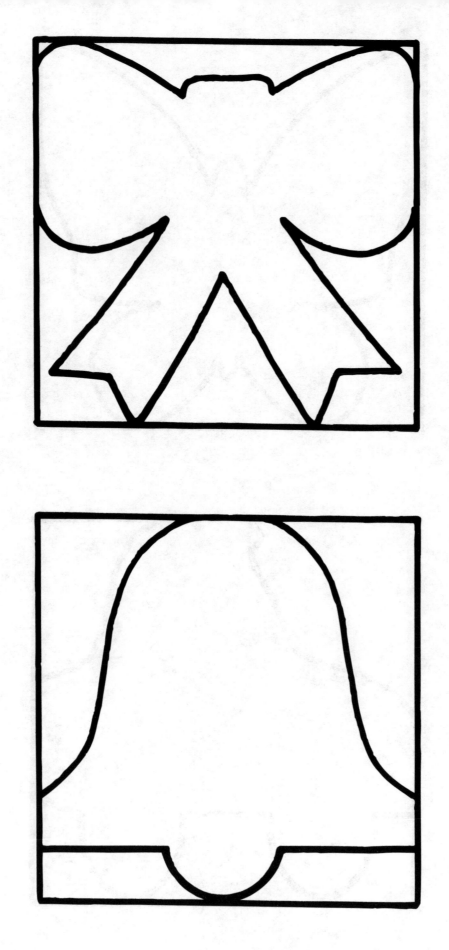

10

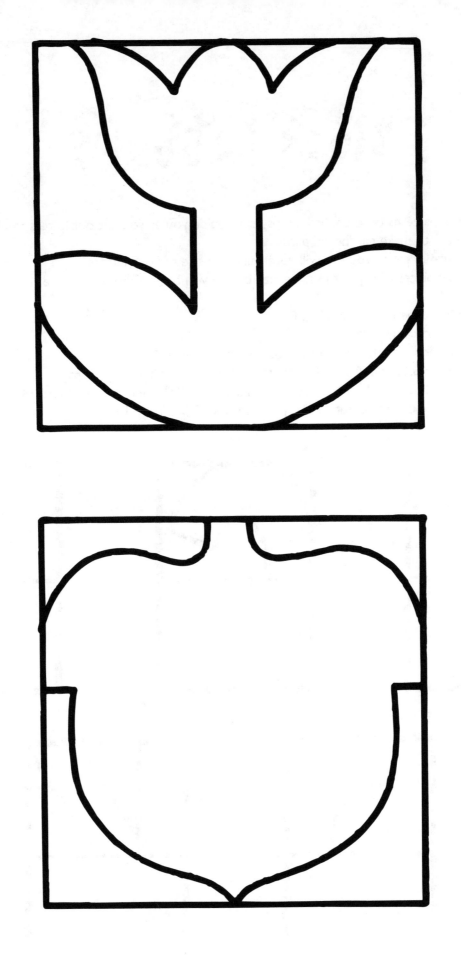

11

Block Letters

Use the patterns on the following pages to guide you as you cut out letters freehand, or use them to make cardboard patterns.

* The size of paper you use will determine the size of your letters.
* Cut all pieces of paper the same size before you begin. Corners may be rounded, if you prefer.
* For F, cut the lower leg off an E.
* For G, add a tip to a C.
* For Q, add a slanted tip to the bottom corner of an O.
* Cut E, C, B, D, and K on a horizontal fold. See the bottom of this page.
* Cut A, H, T, N, O, U, V, W, X, and Y on a vertical fold. See pages 13 and 14.
* Do not fold when cutting I, P, L, J, N, R, S, and Z. See page 14.

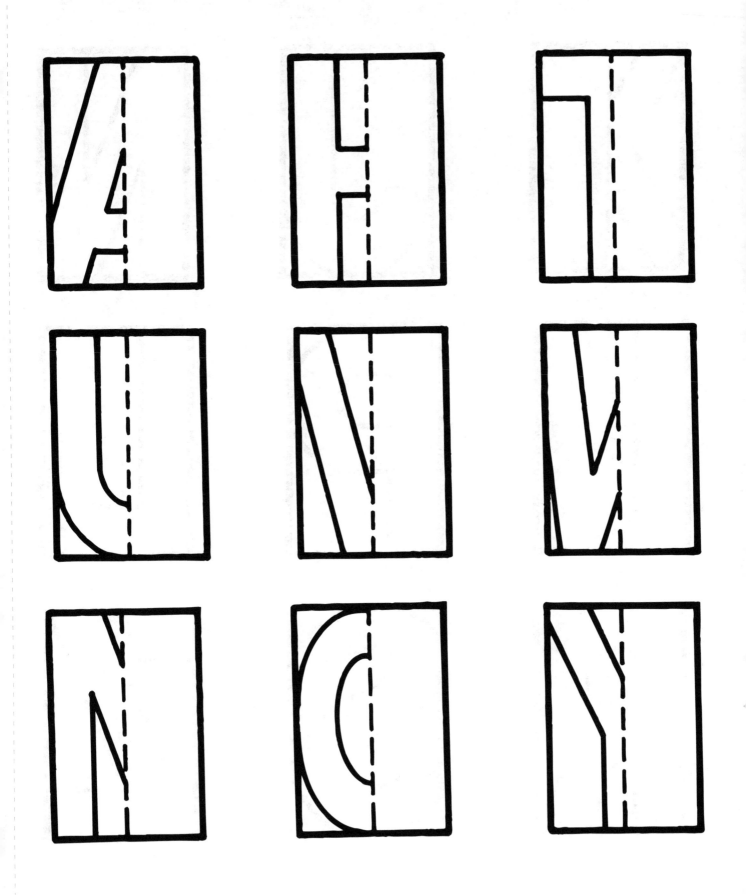

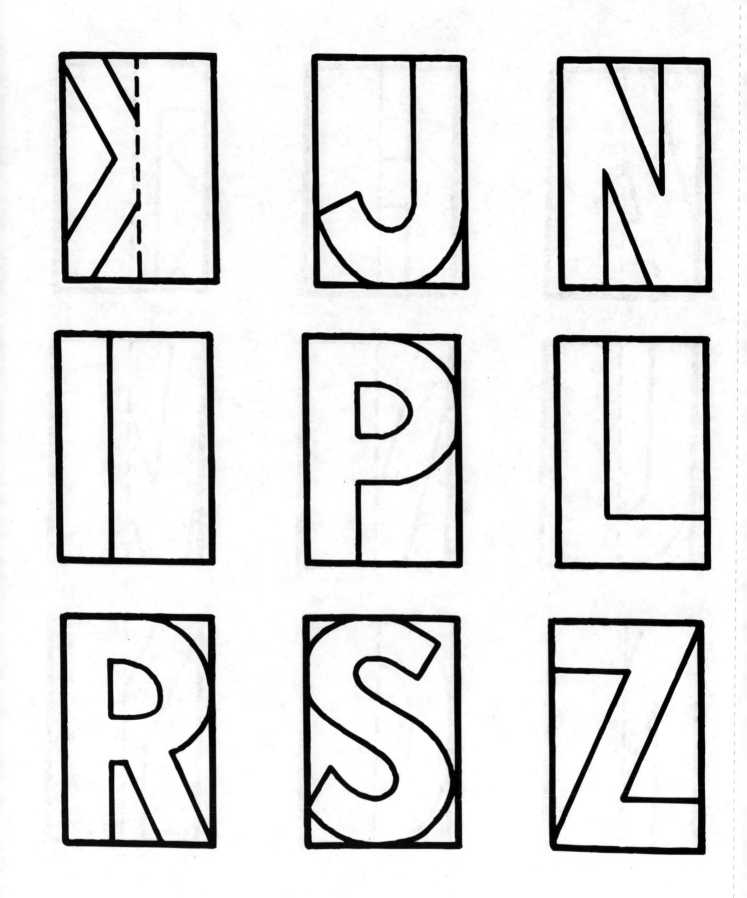

14

15

16

17

18

19

20

21

22

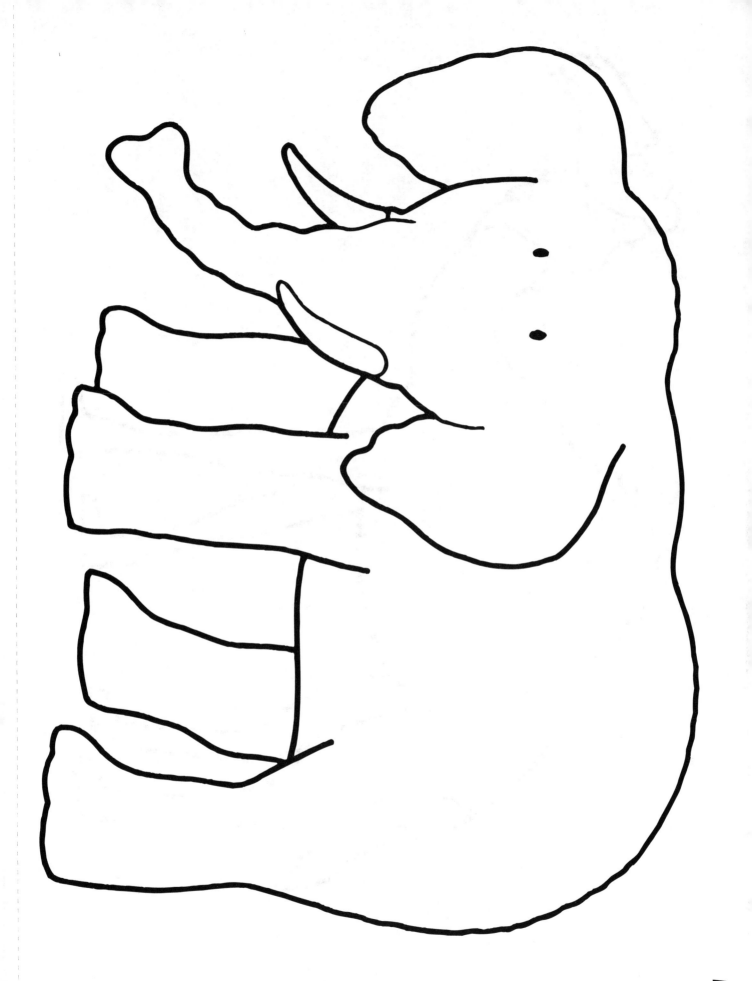

23

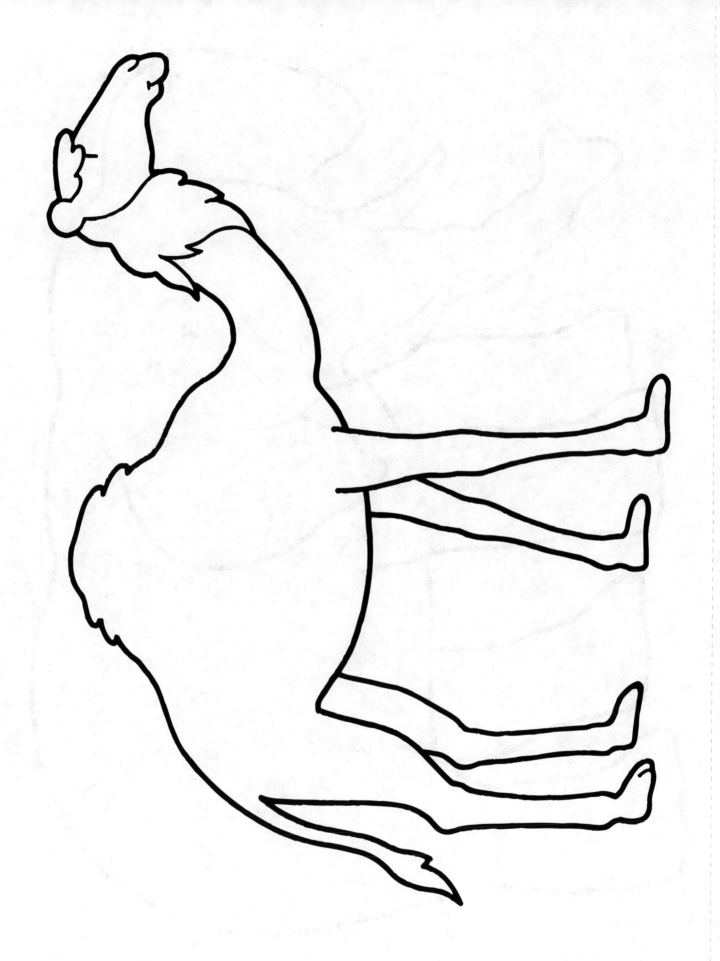

24

2⁵

26

27

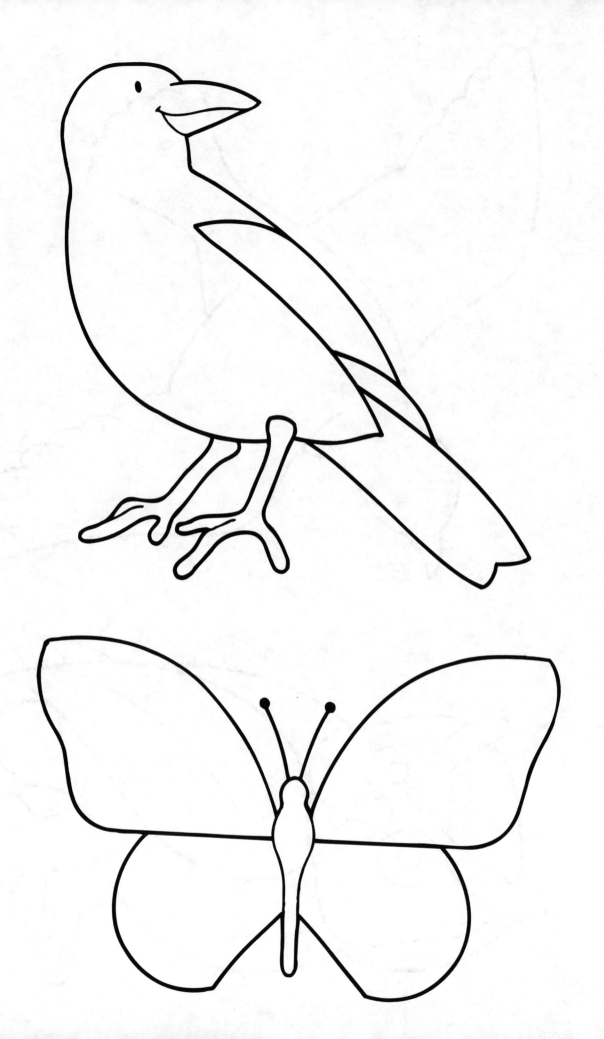

28

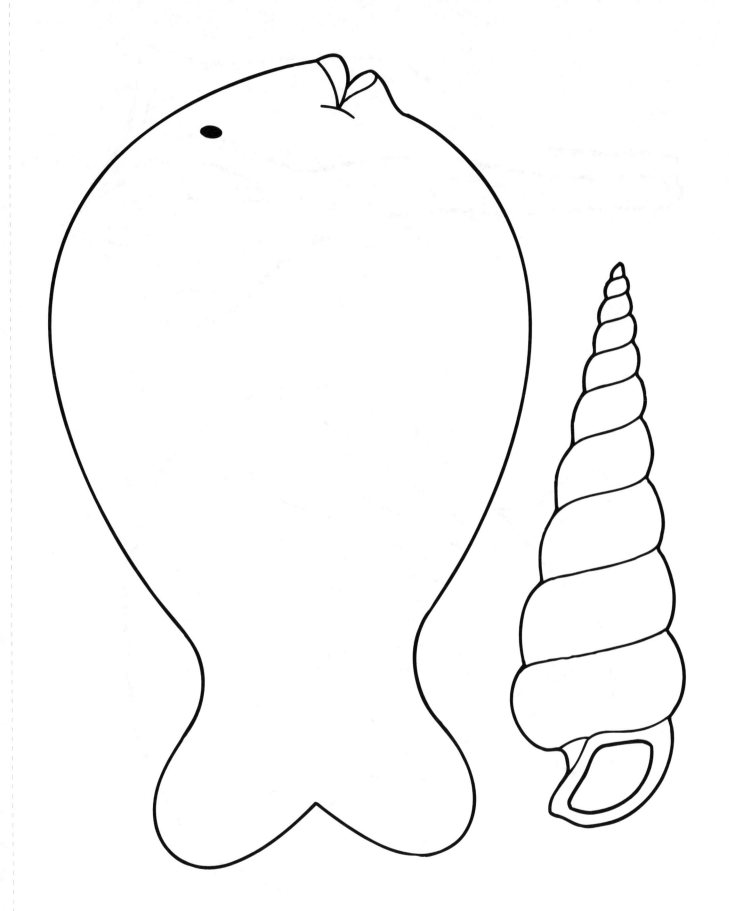

29

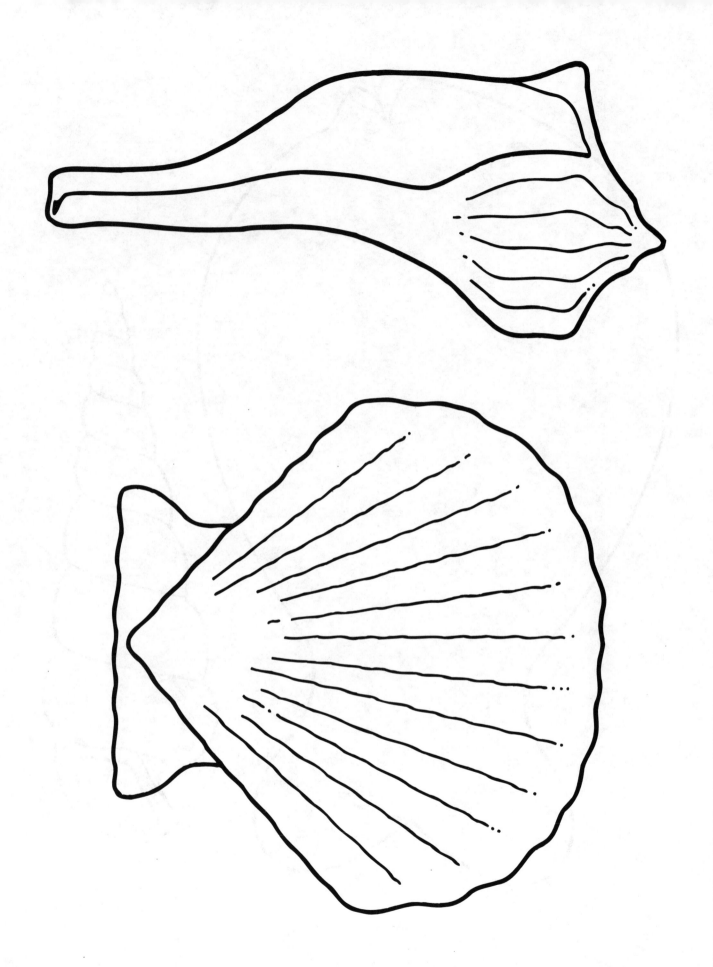

30

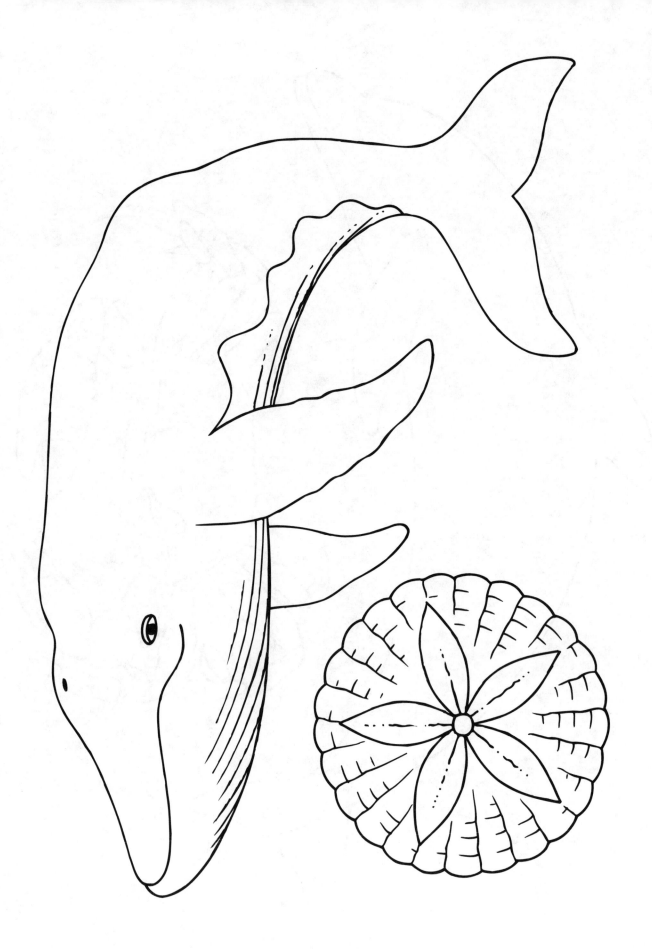

32

33

34

35

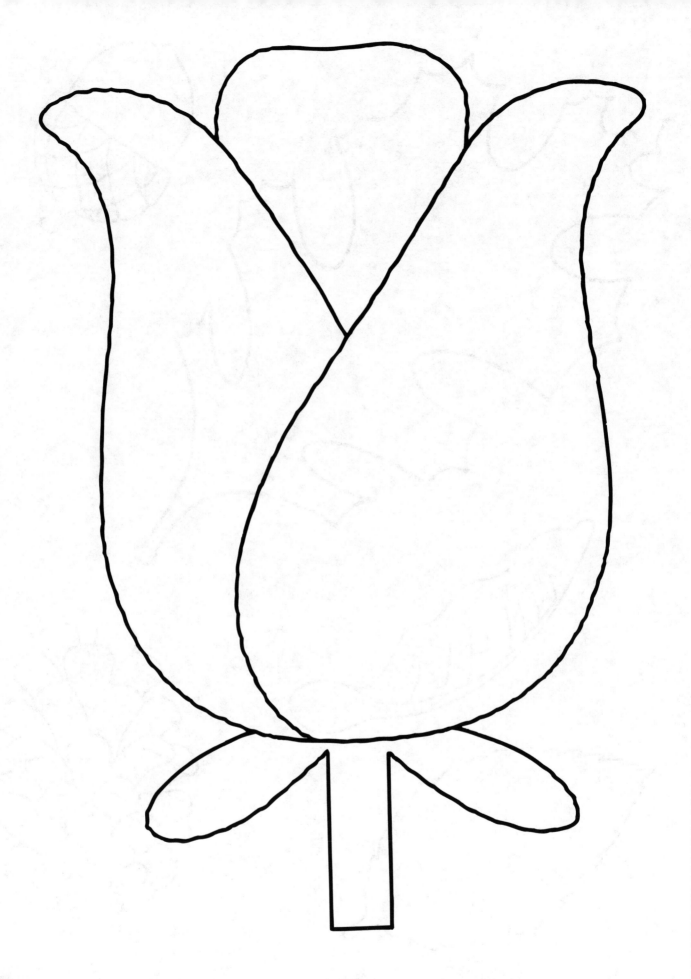

36

37

38

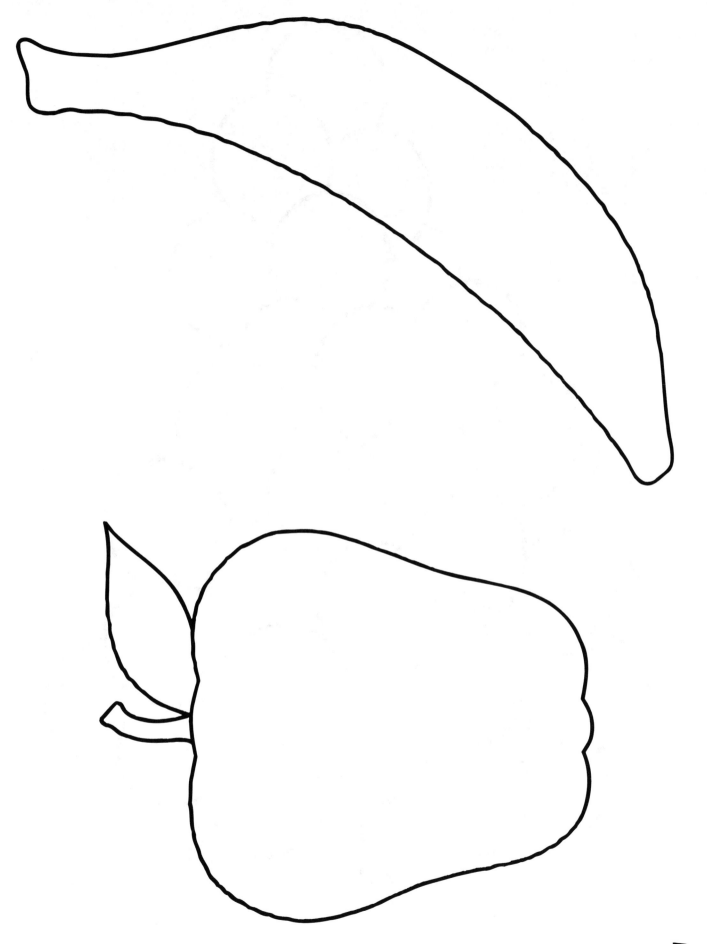

39

40

41

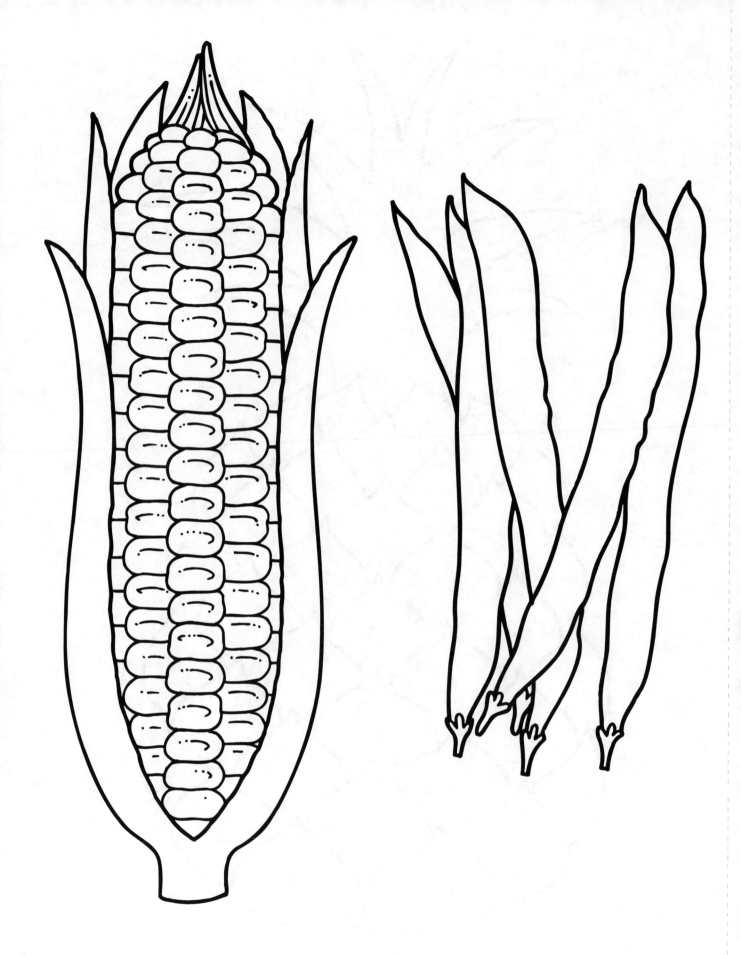

42

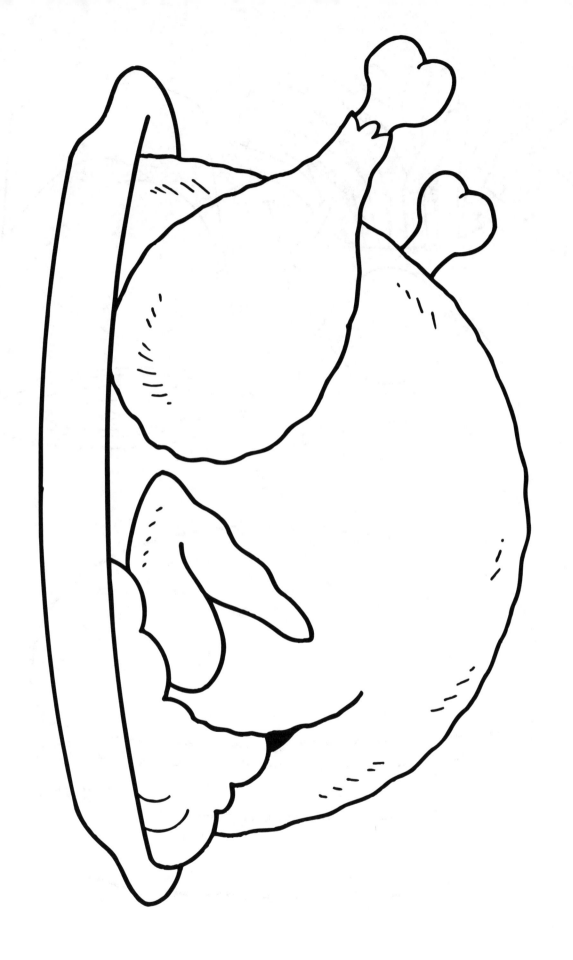

43

45

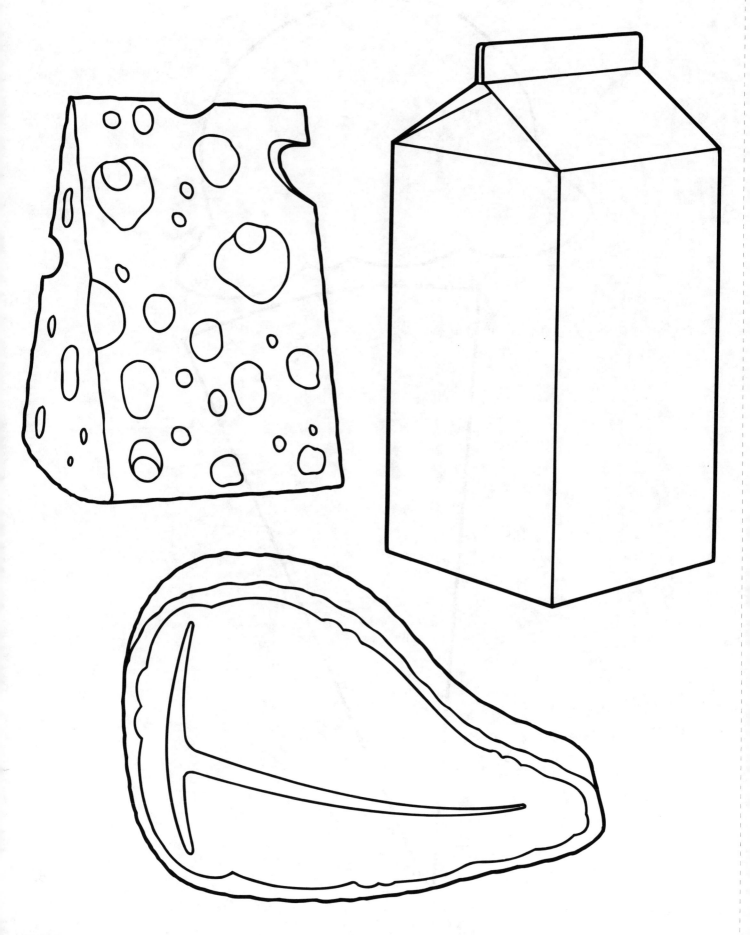

46

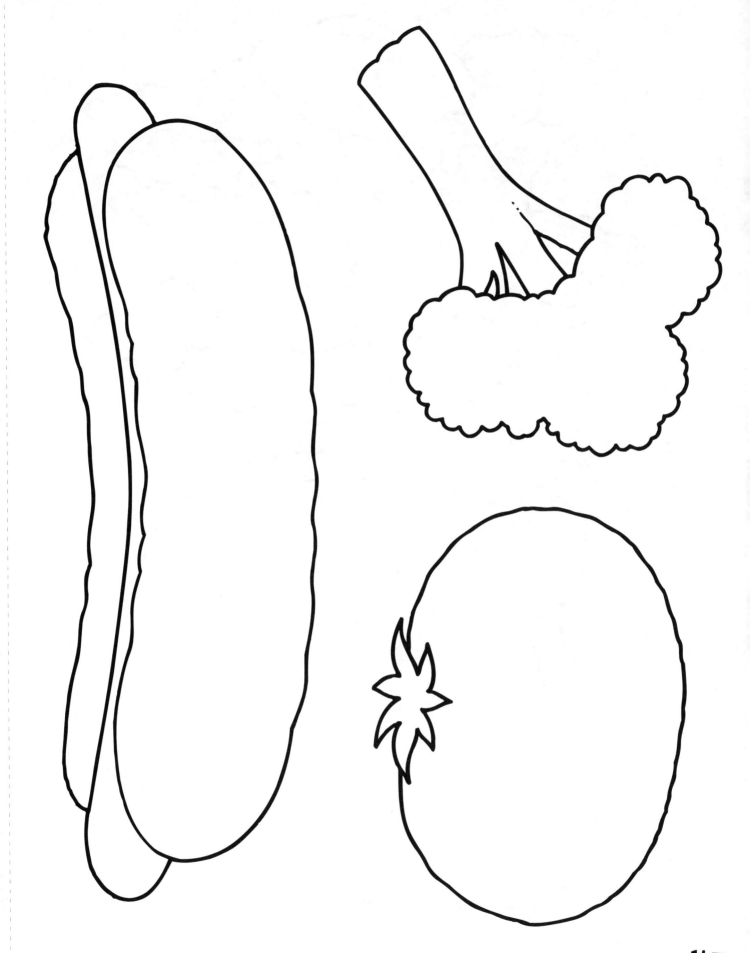

47

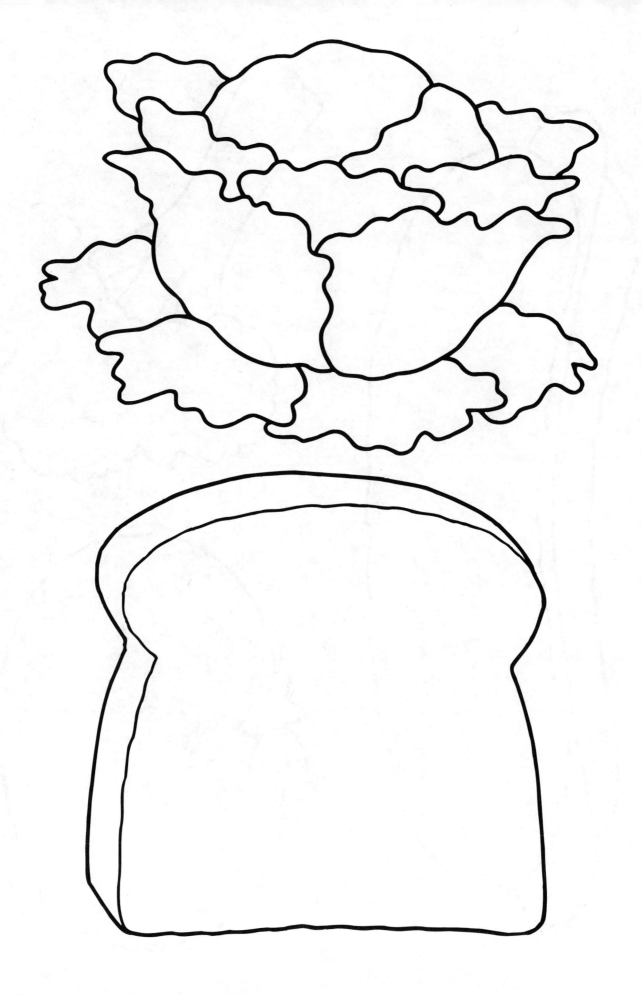

48

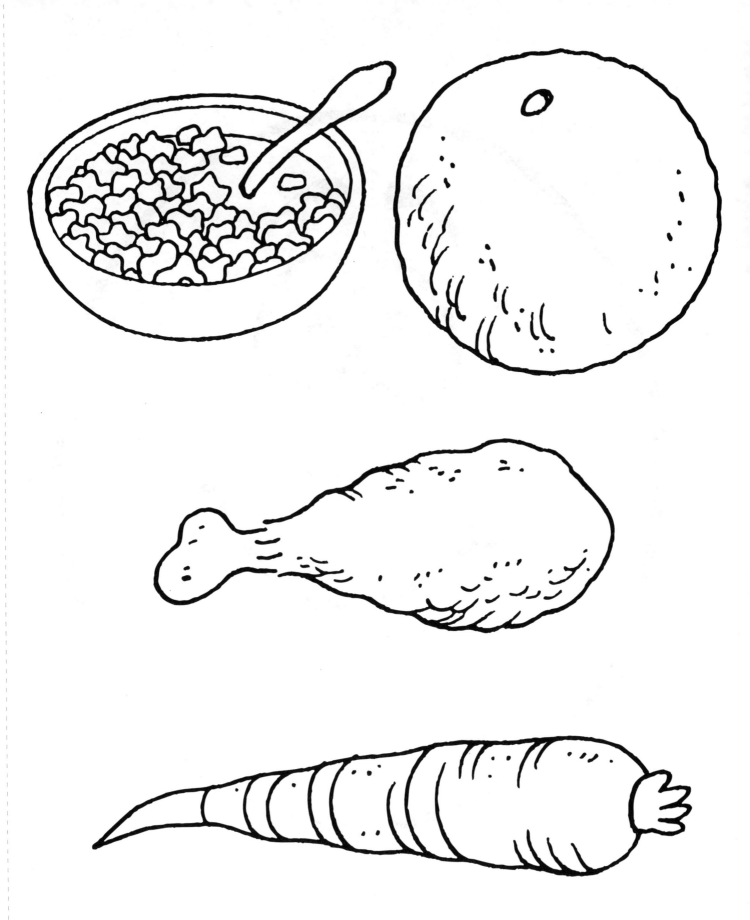

49

50

51

52

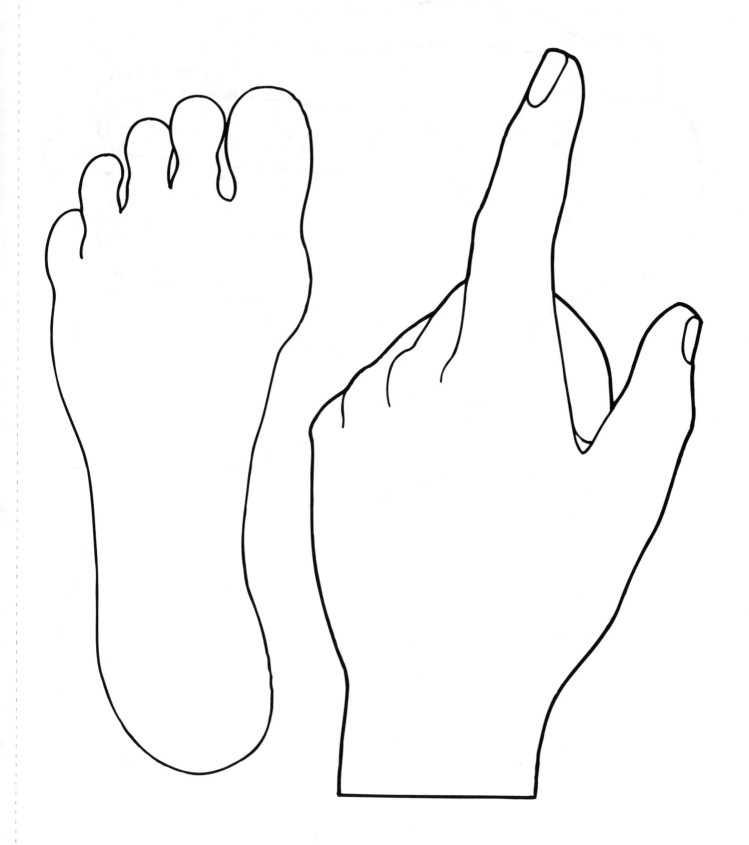

53

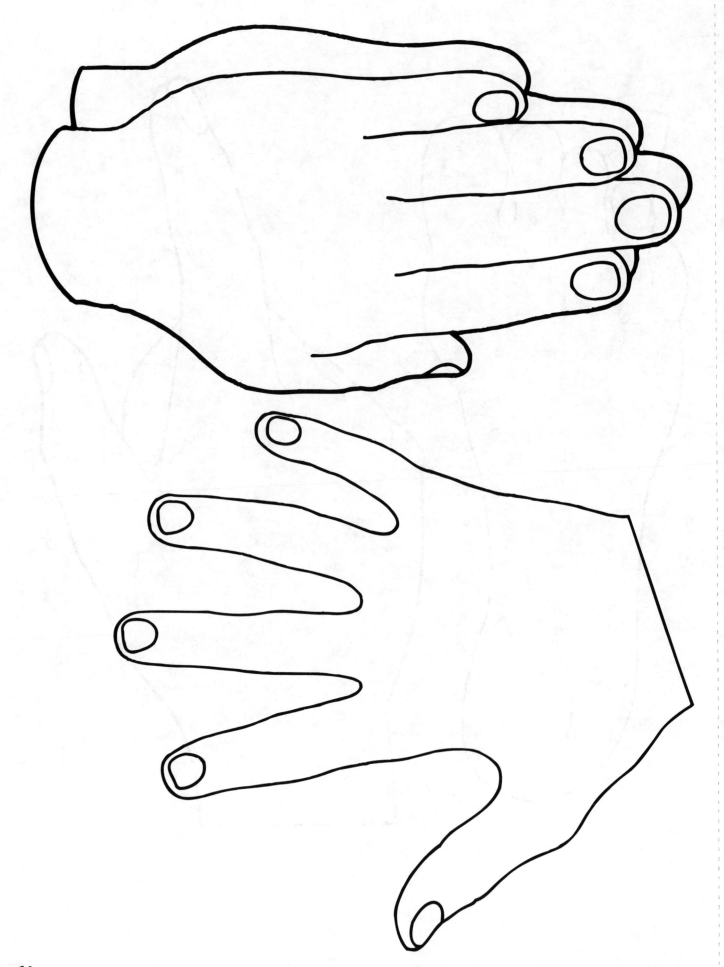

54

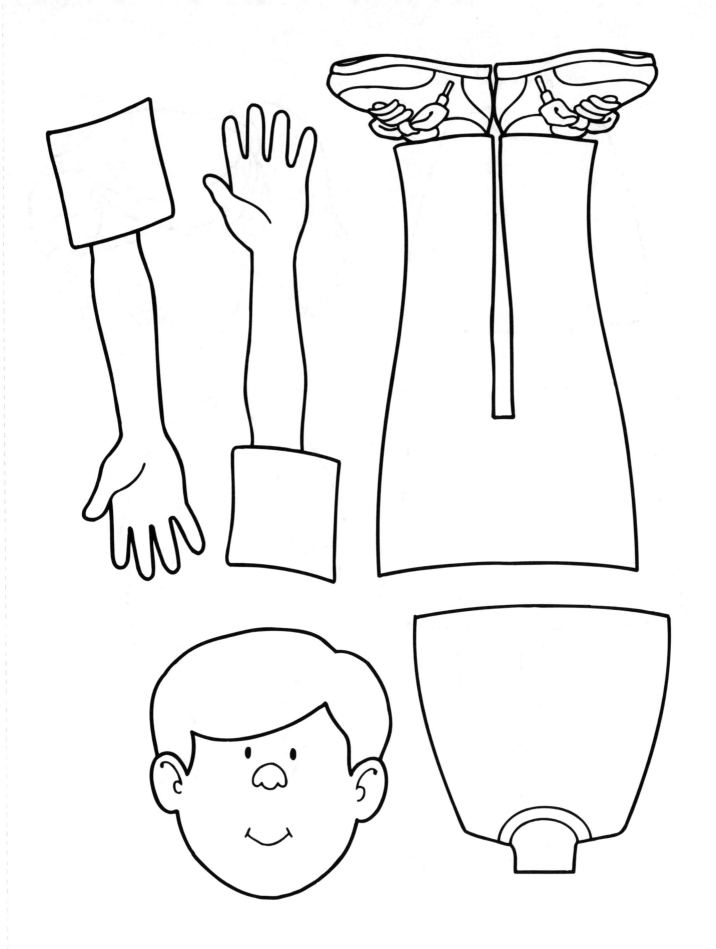

56

58

59

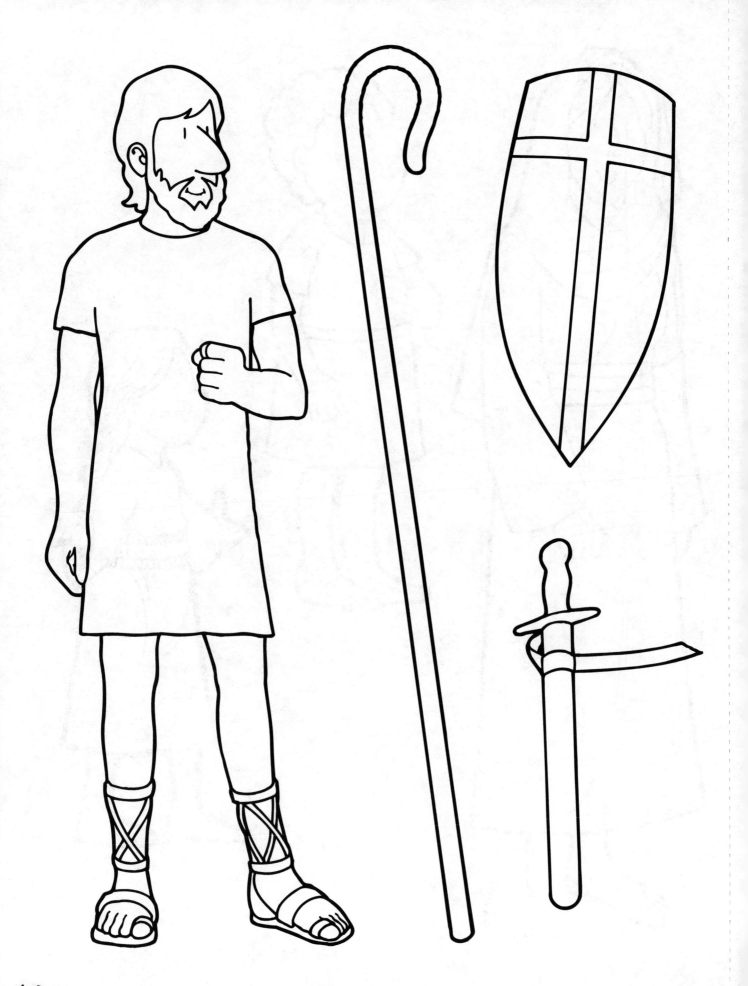

61

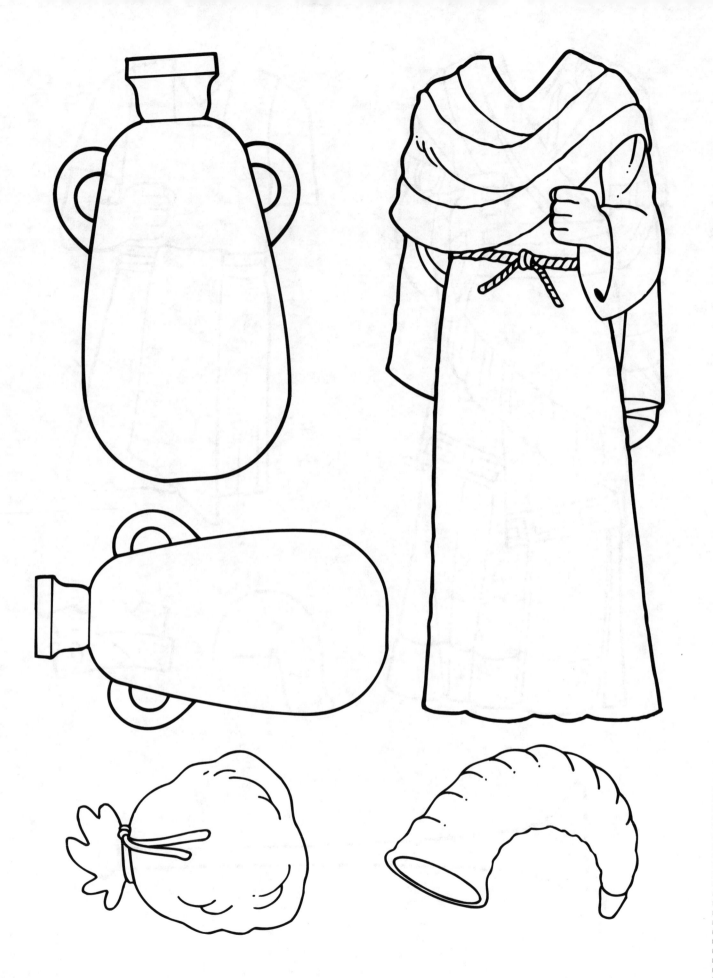

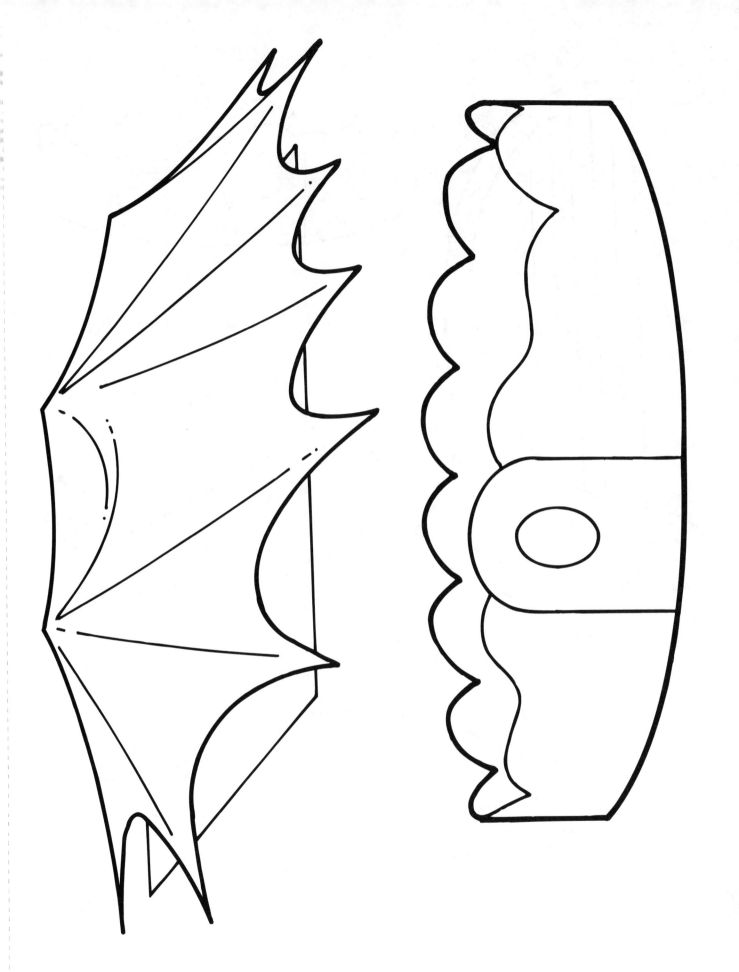

63

64

65

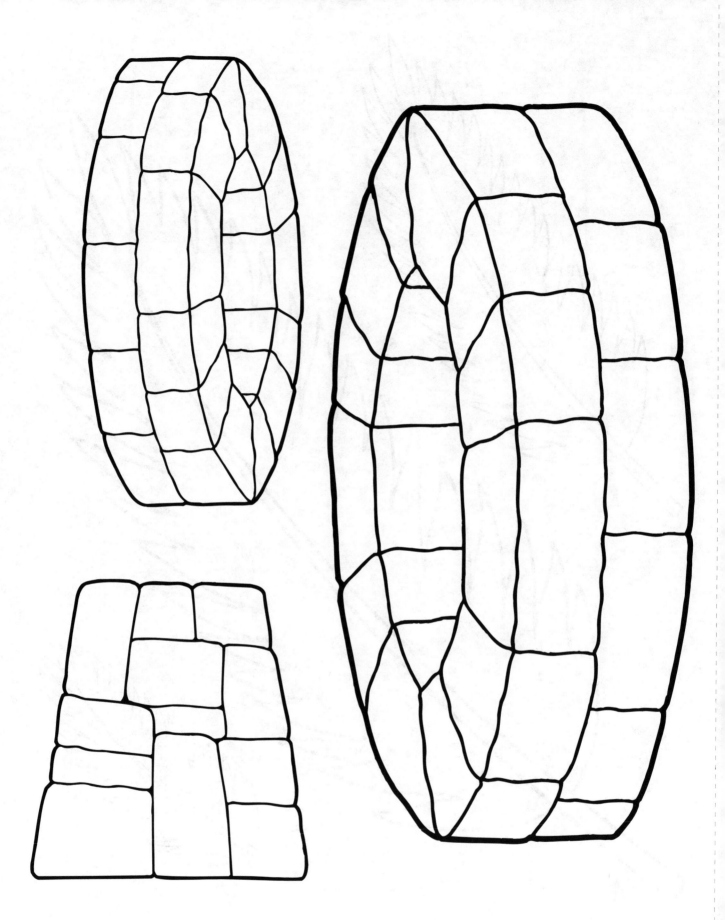

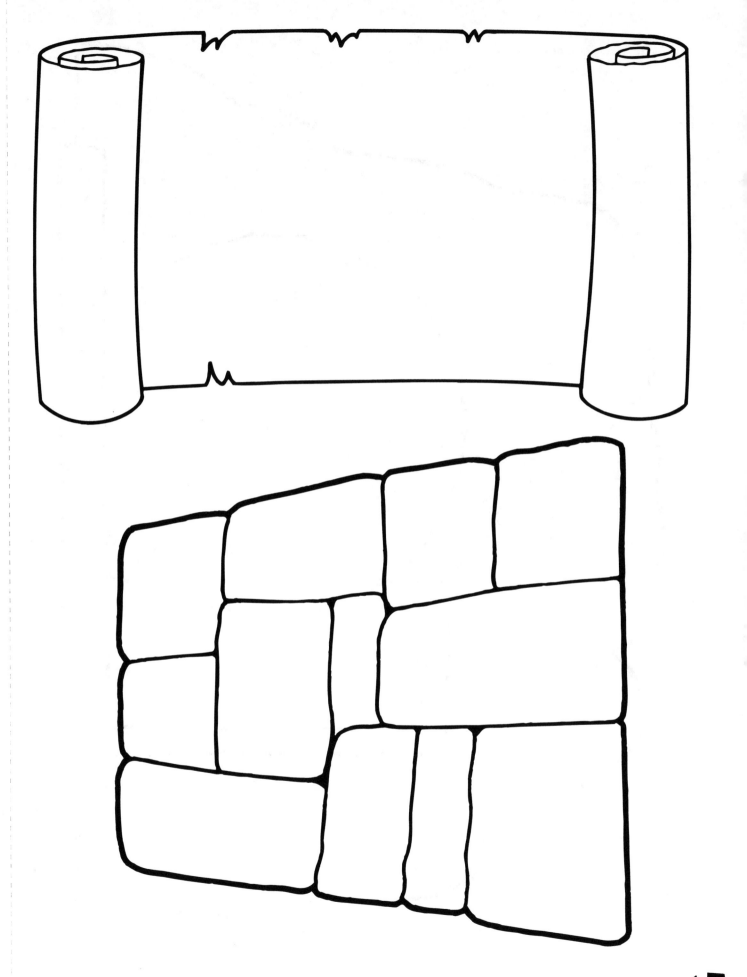

67

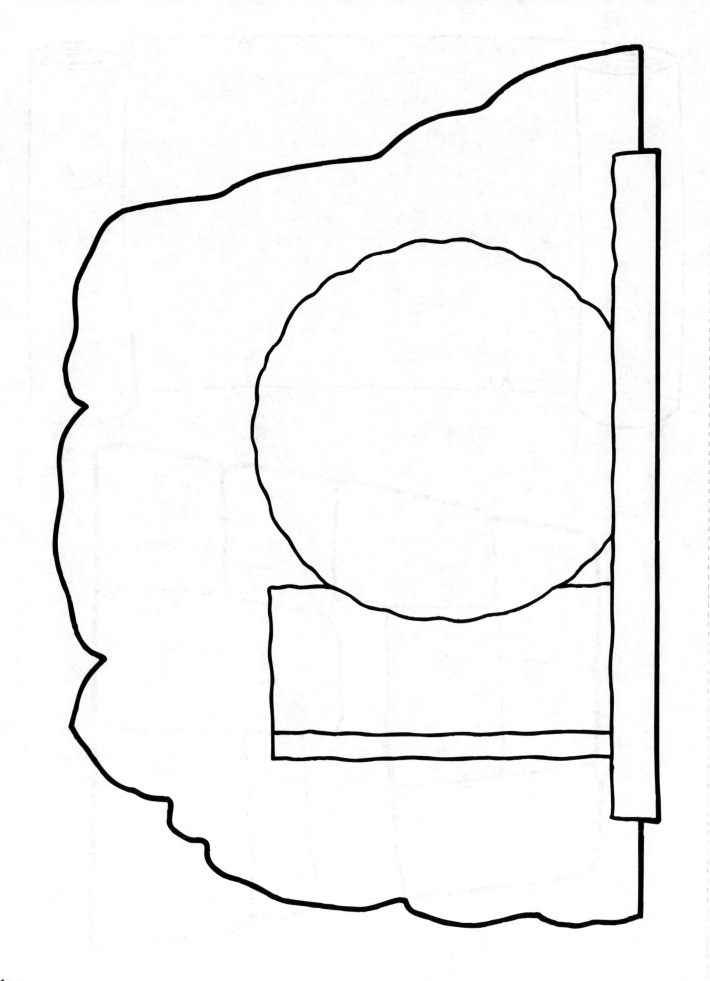

68

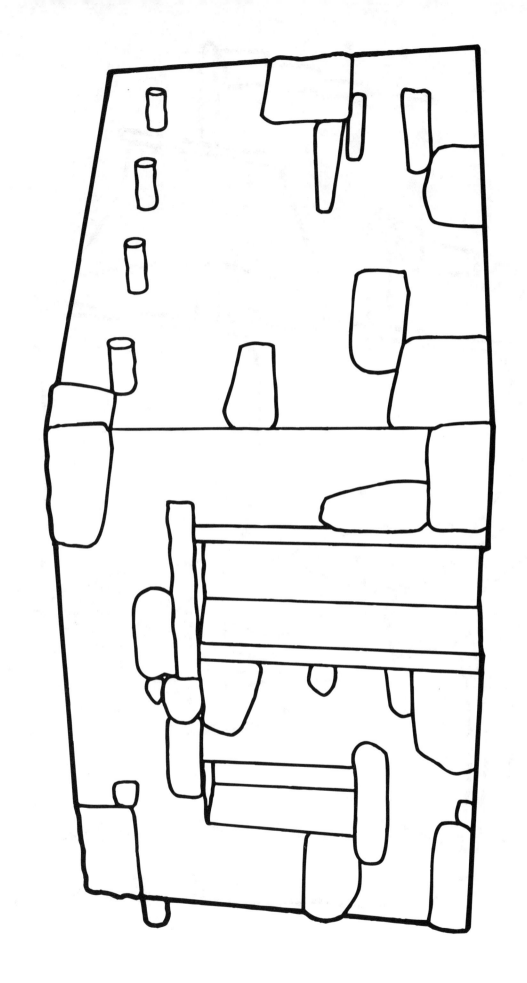

69

70

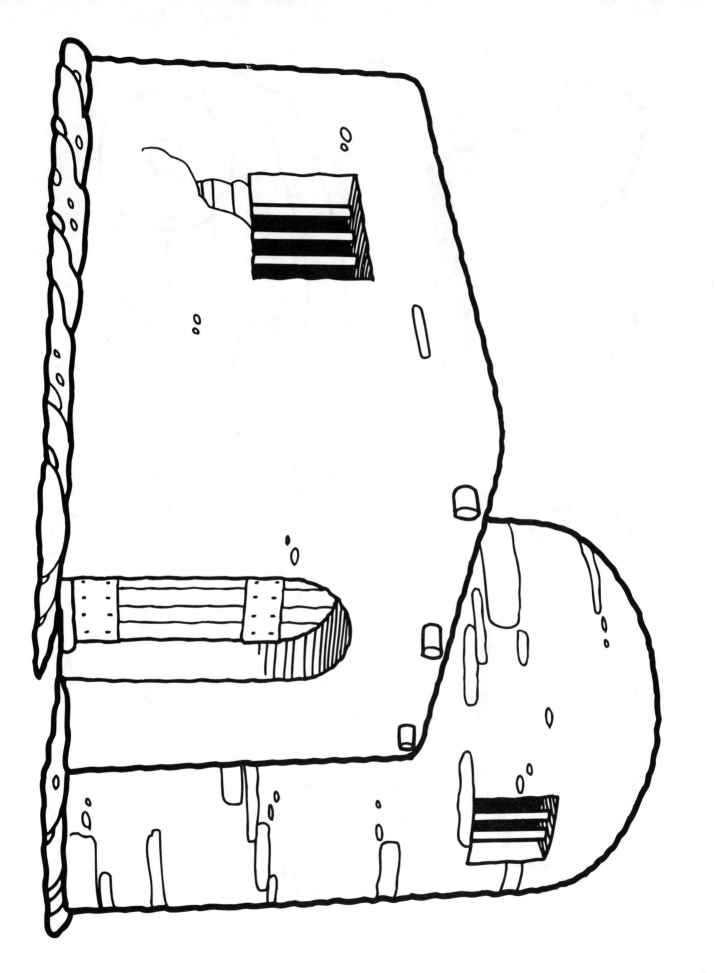

71

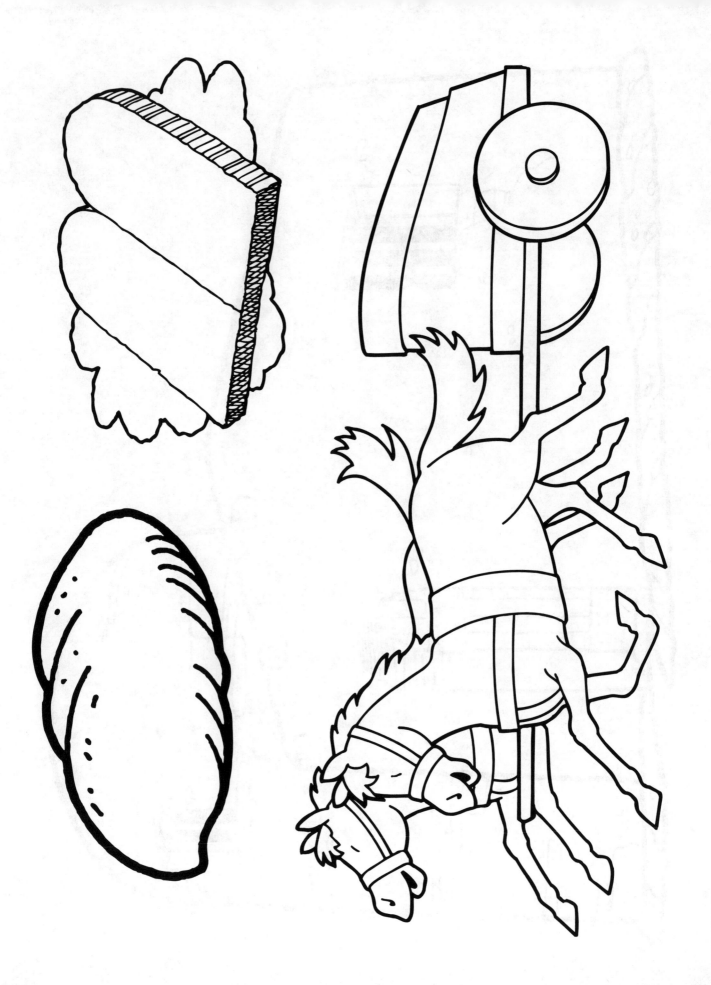

73

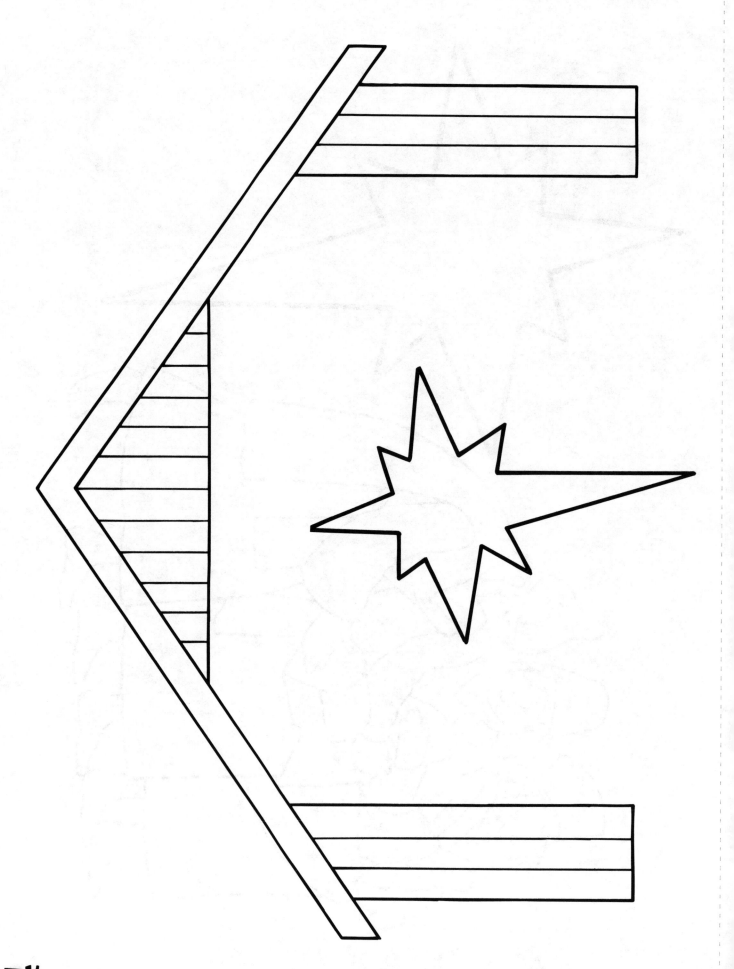

74

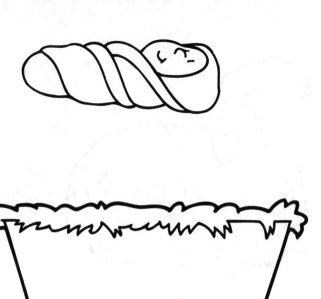

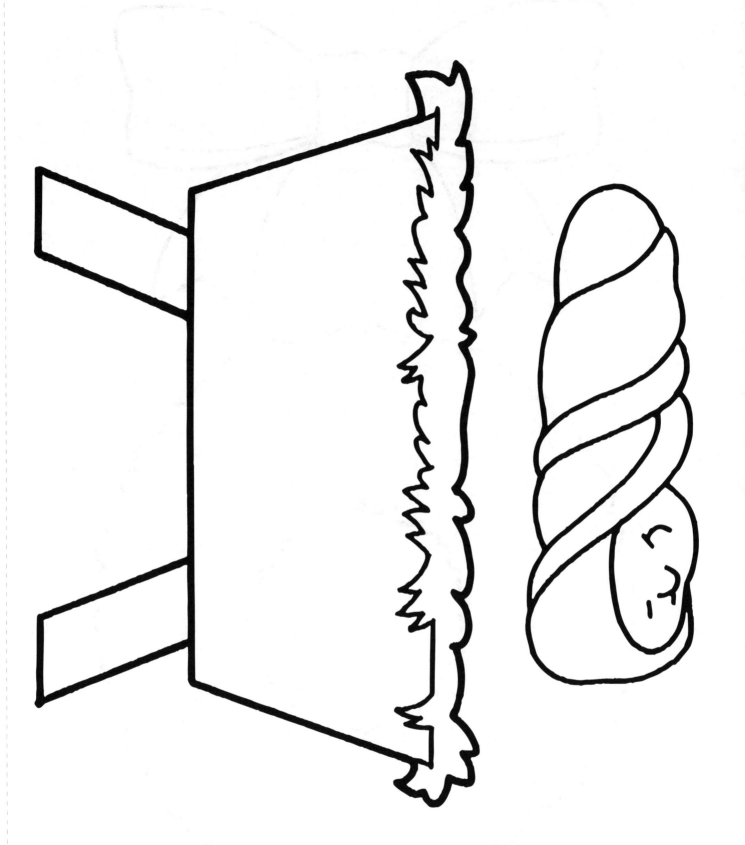

79

81

83

84

85

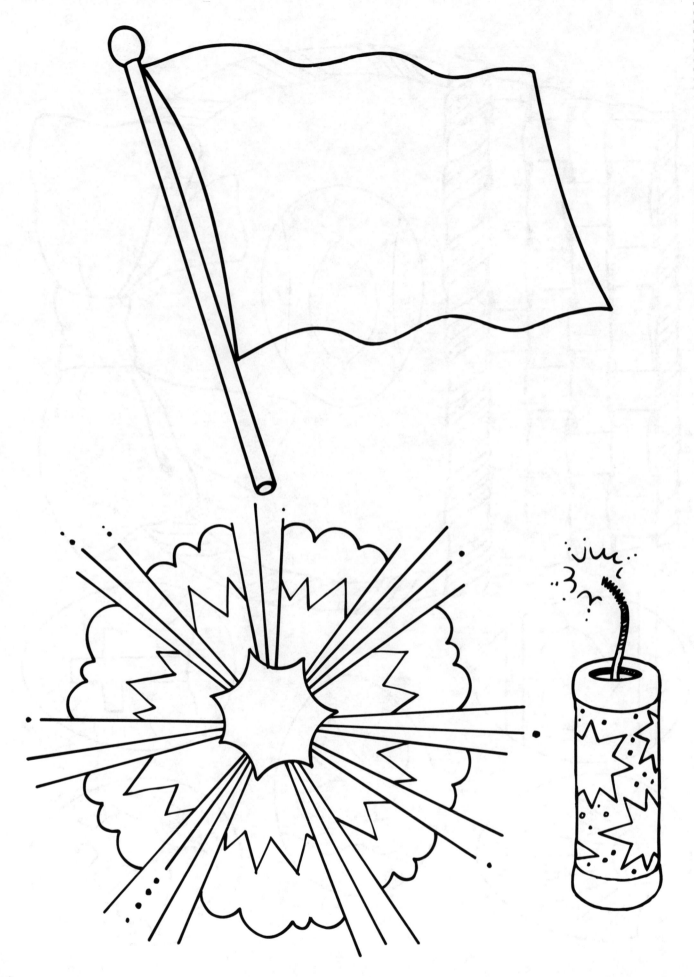

87

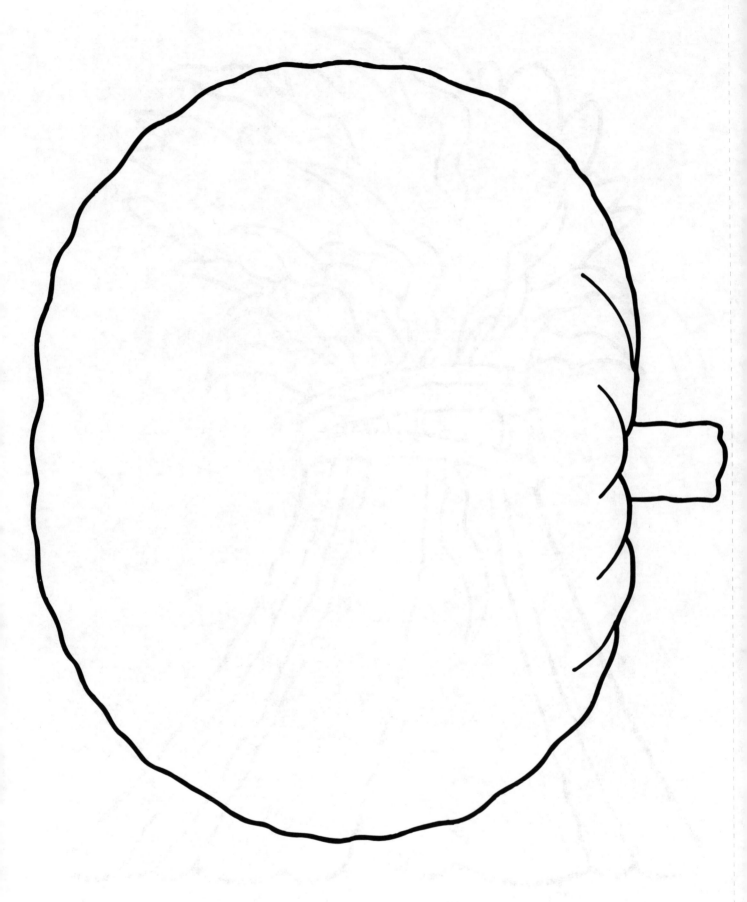

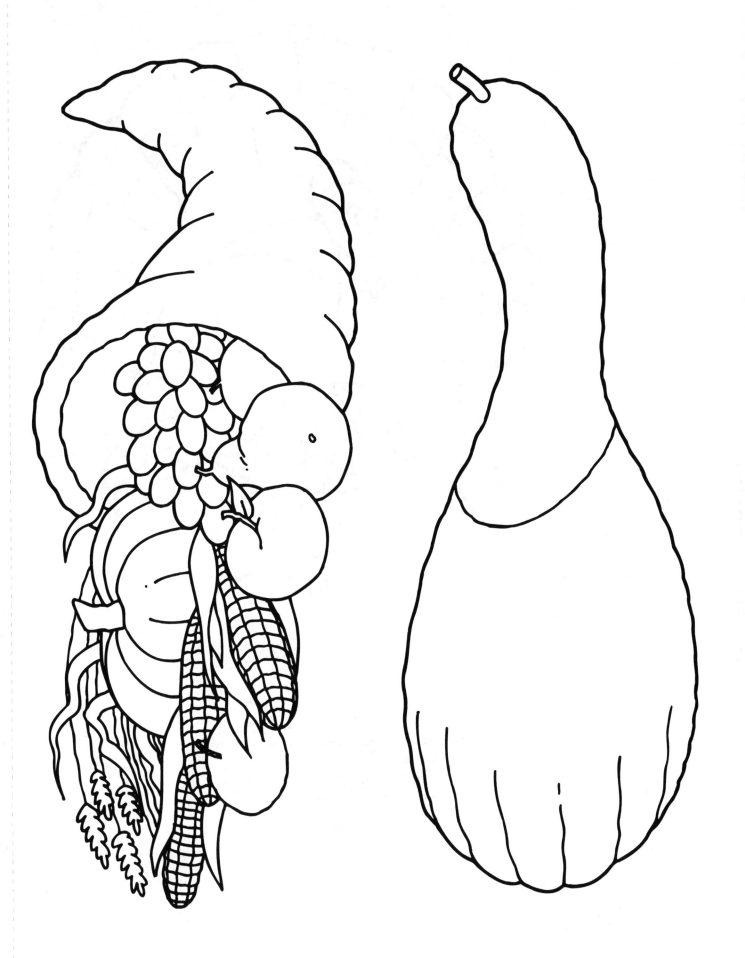

89

91

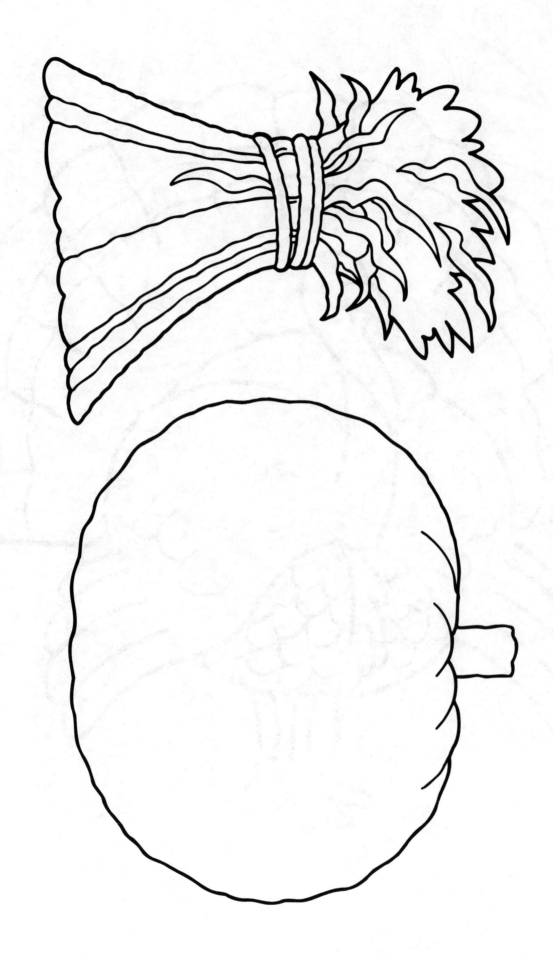

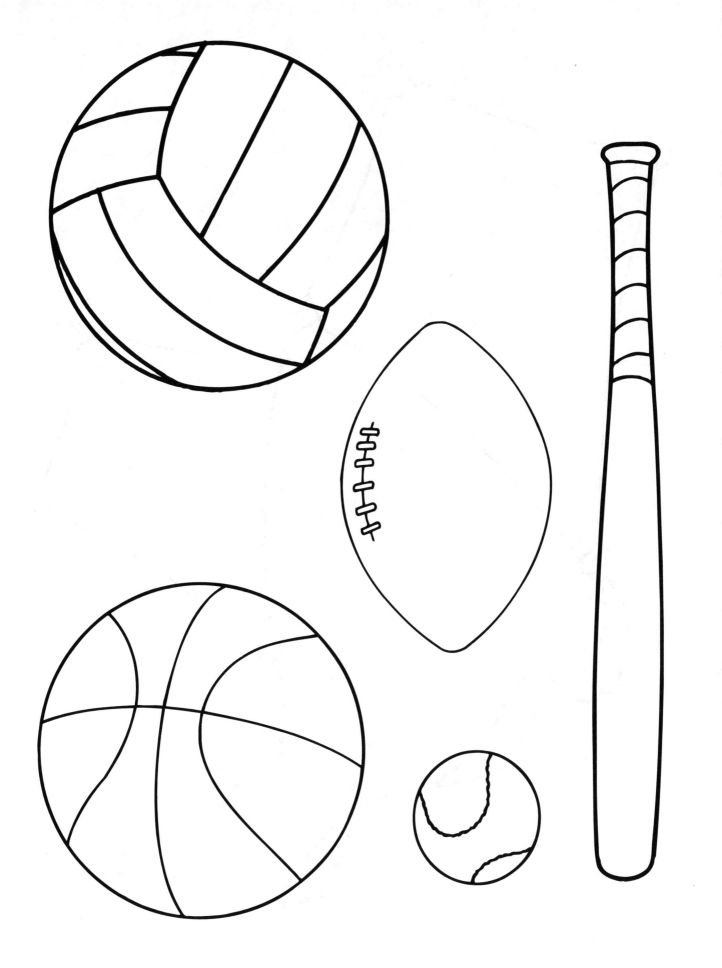

93

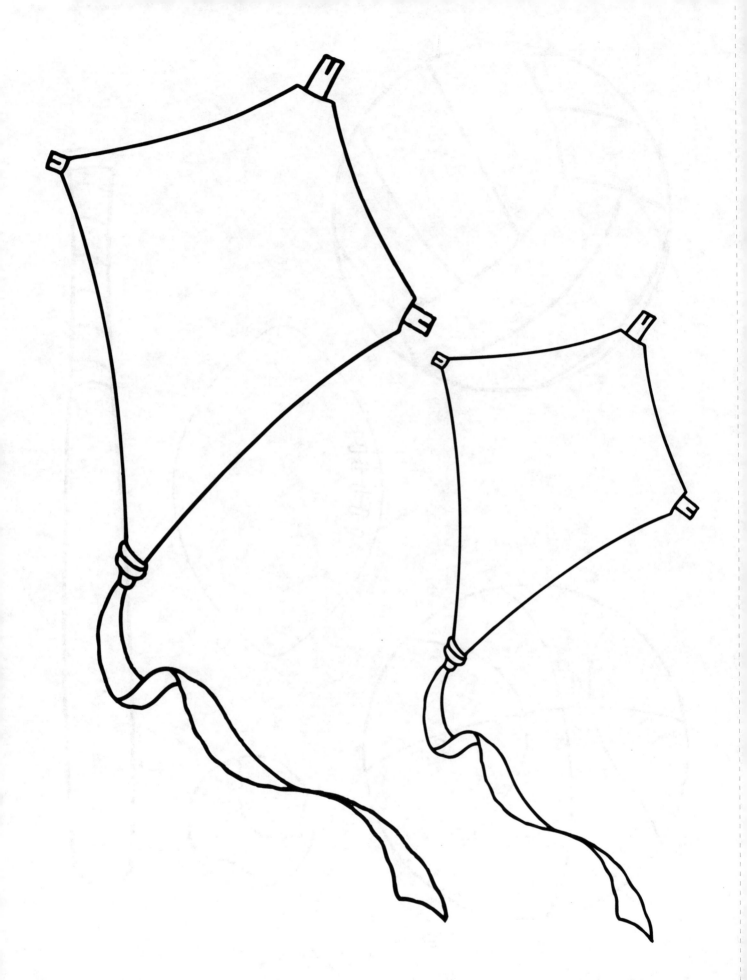

94

95

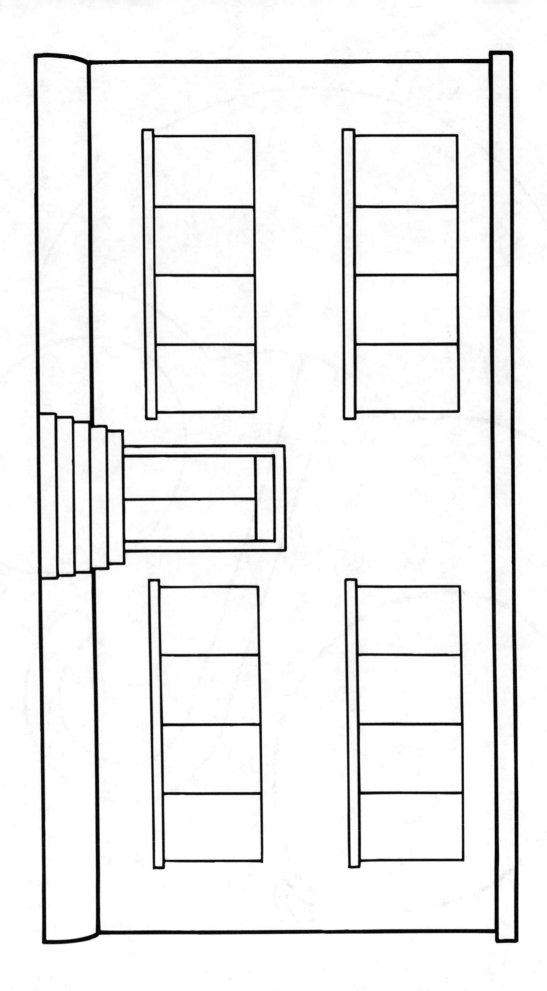

96

97

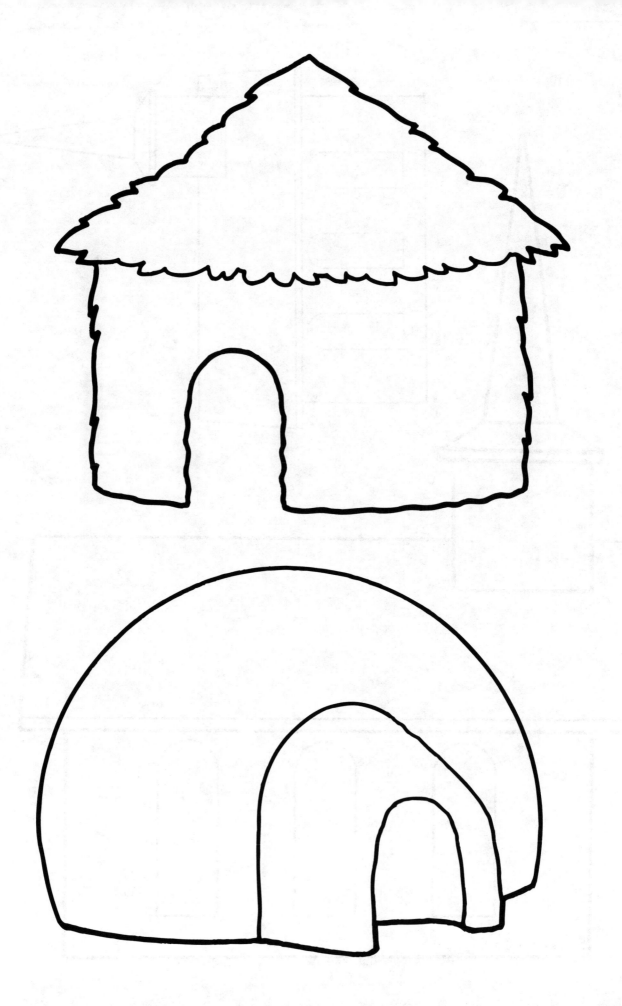

98

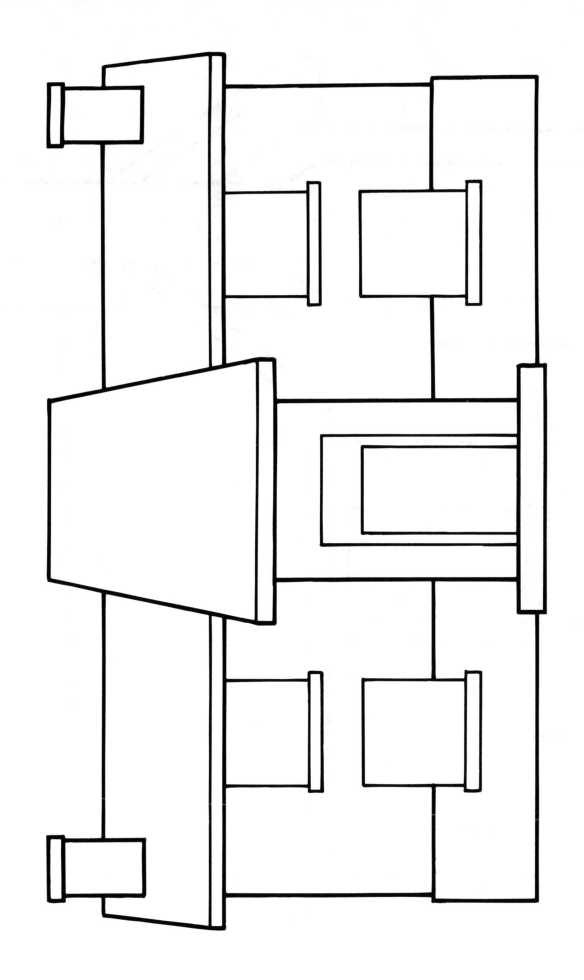

99

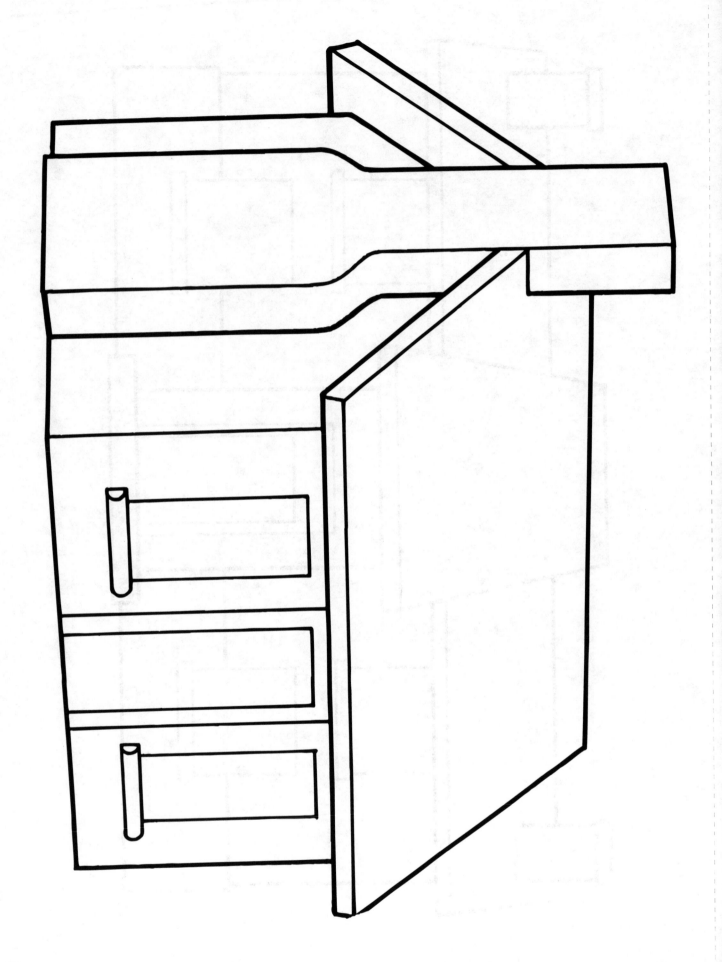

100

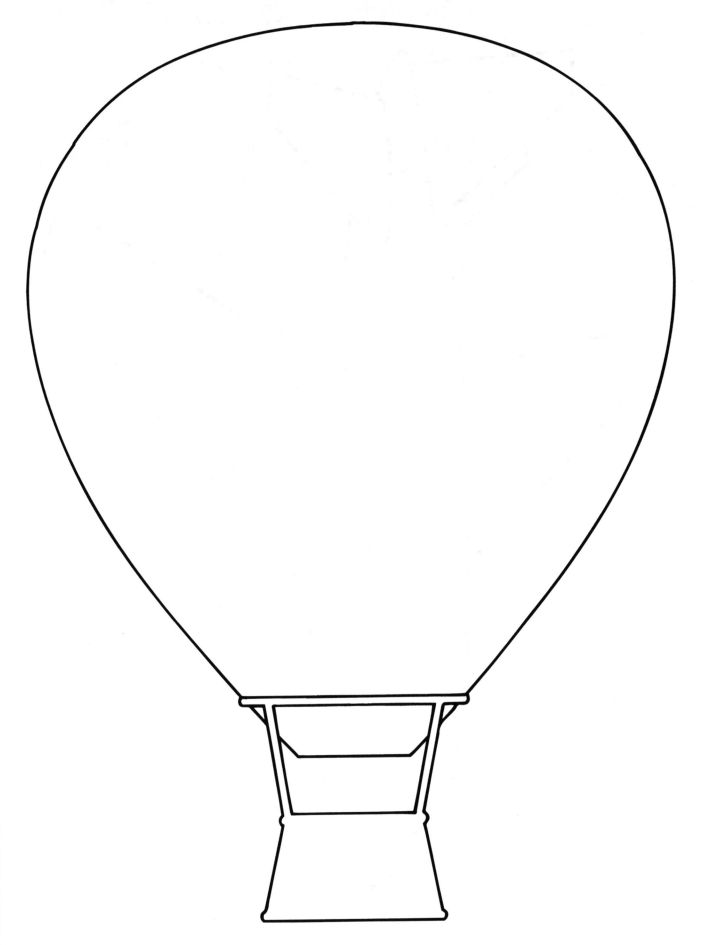

101

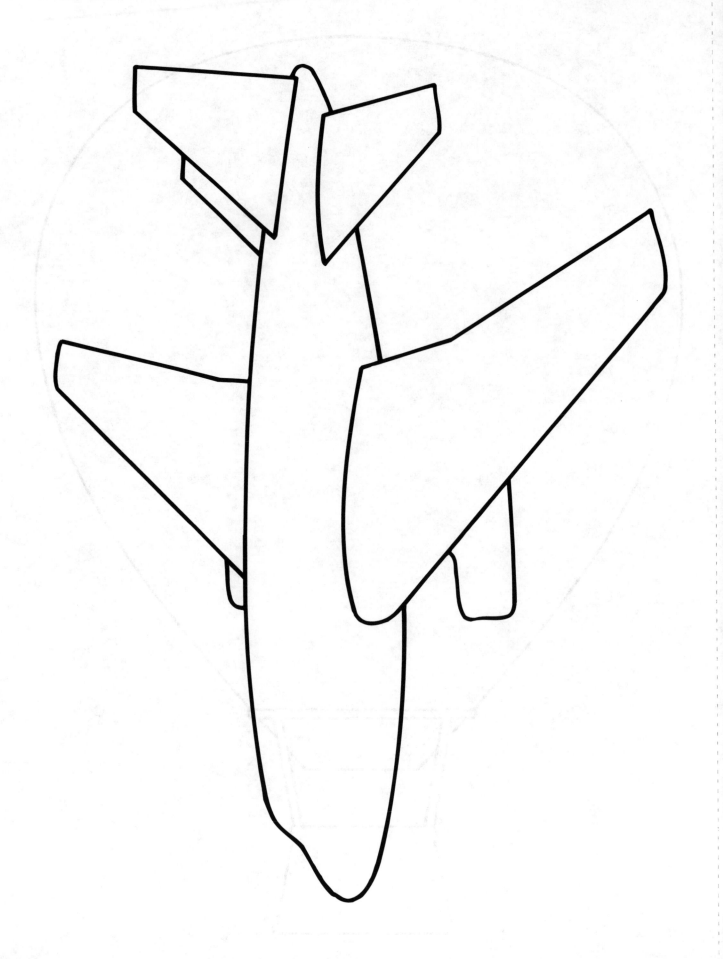

102

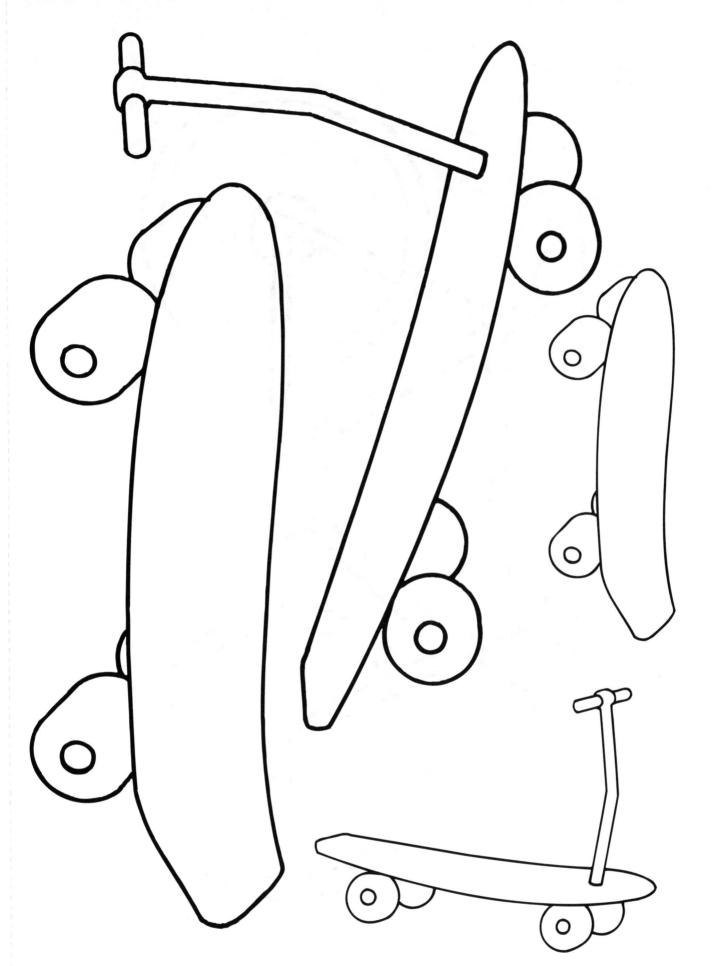

103

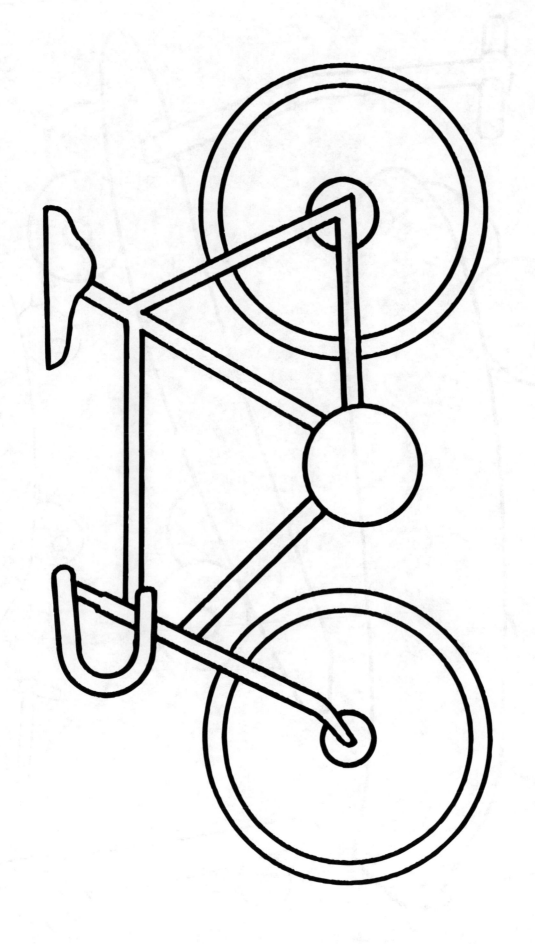

104

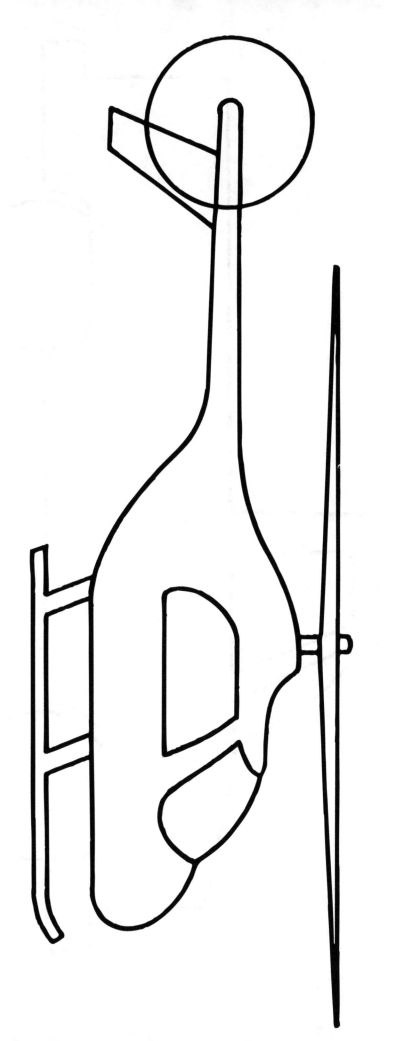

105

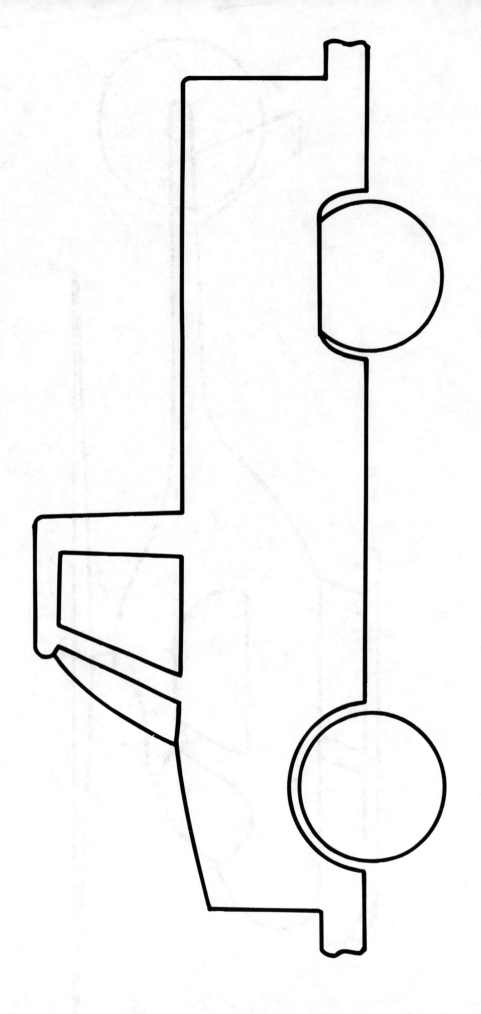

106

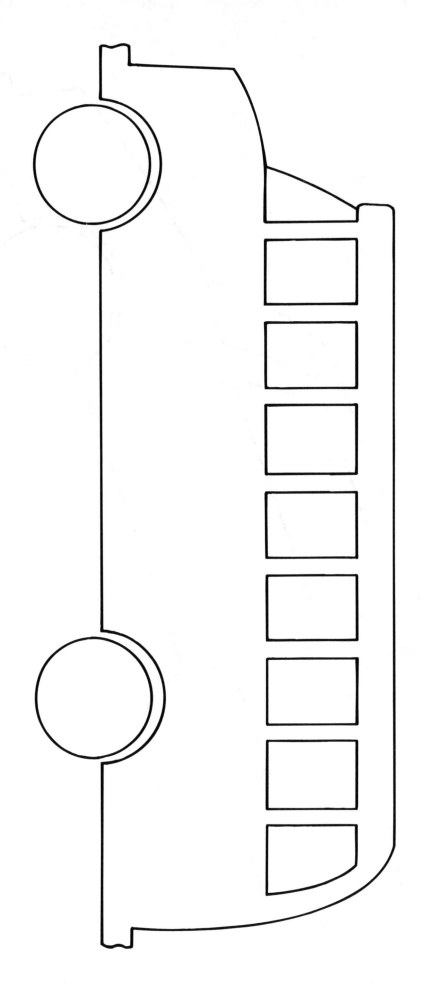

107

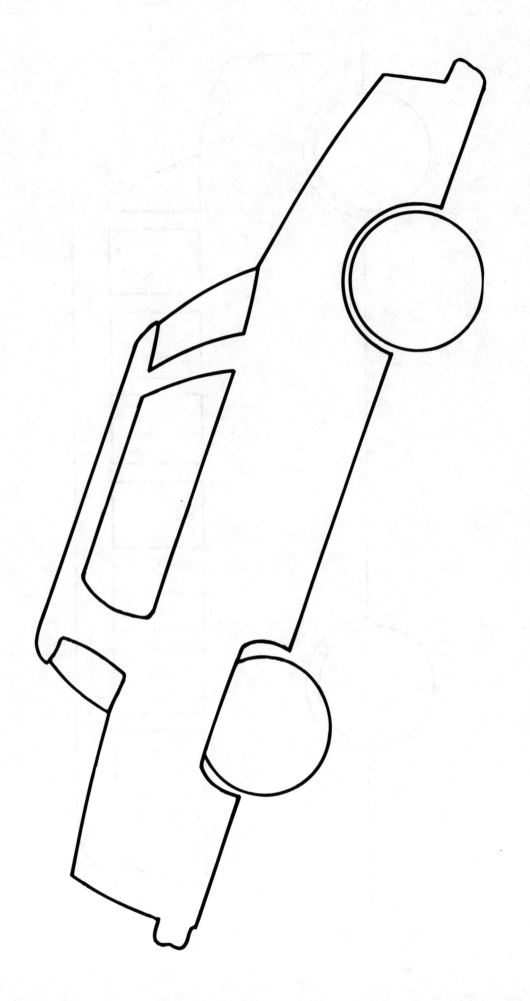

108

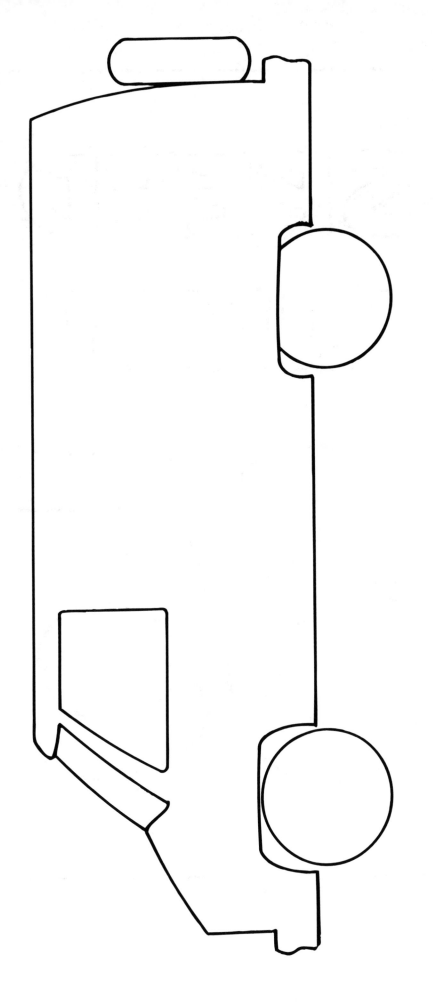

109

SPEED LIMIT 65

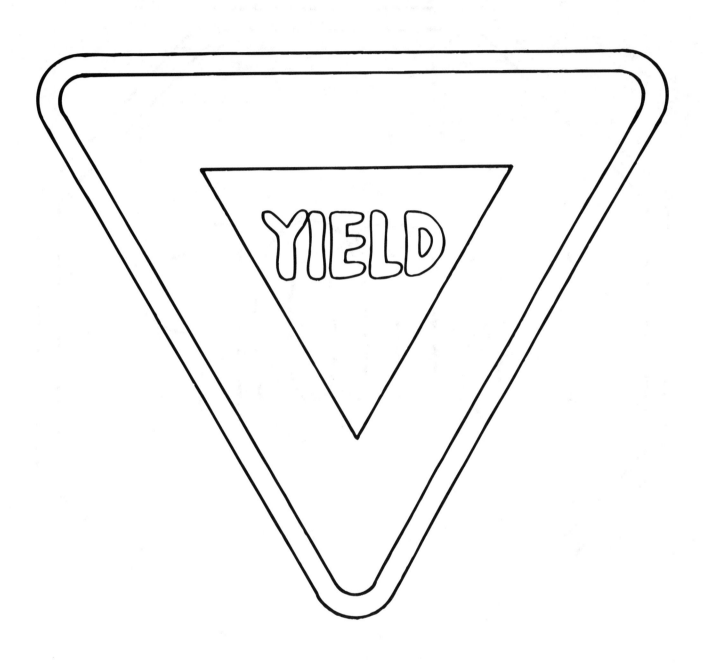

113

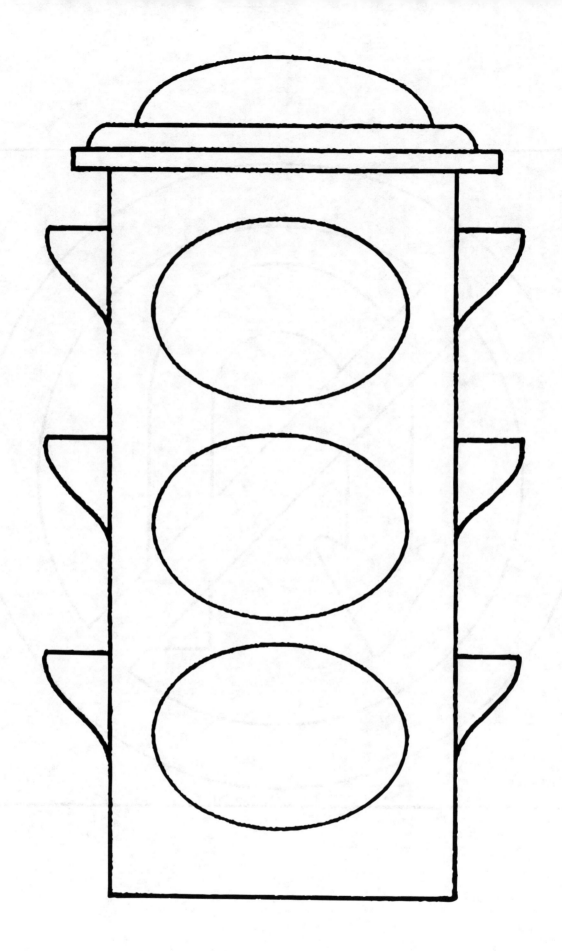

114

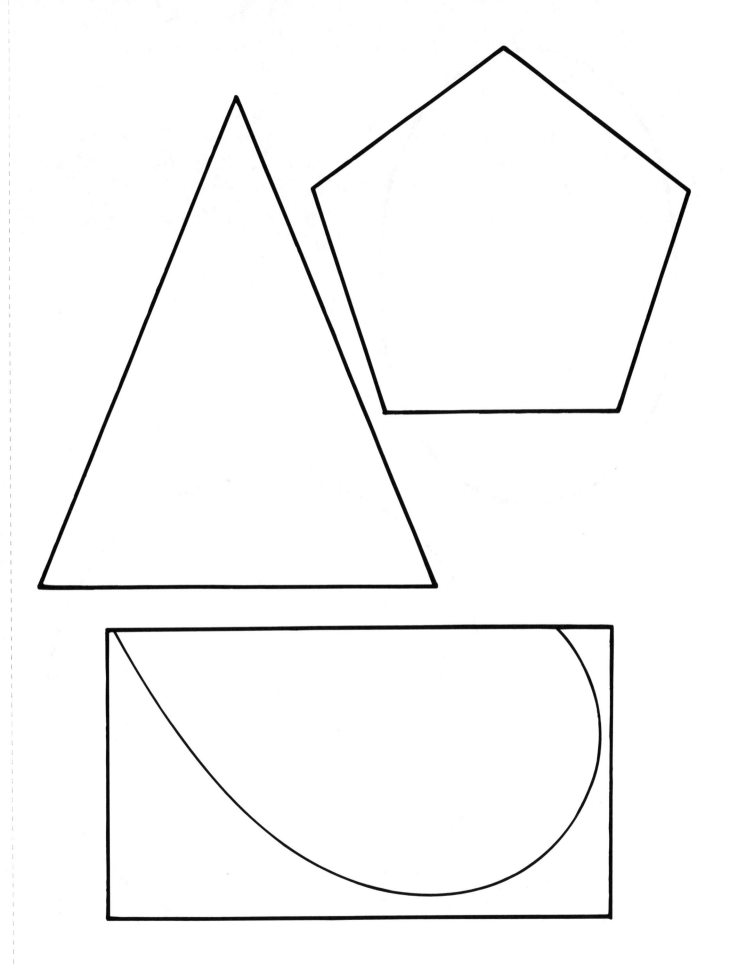

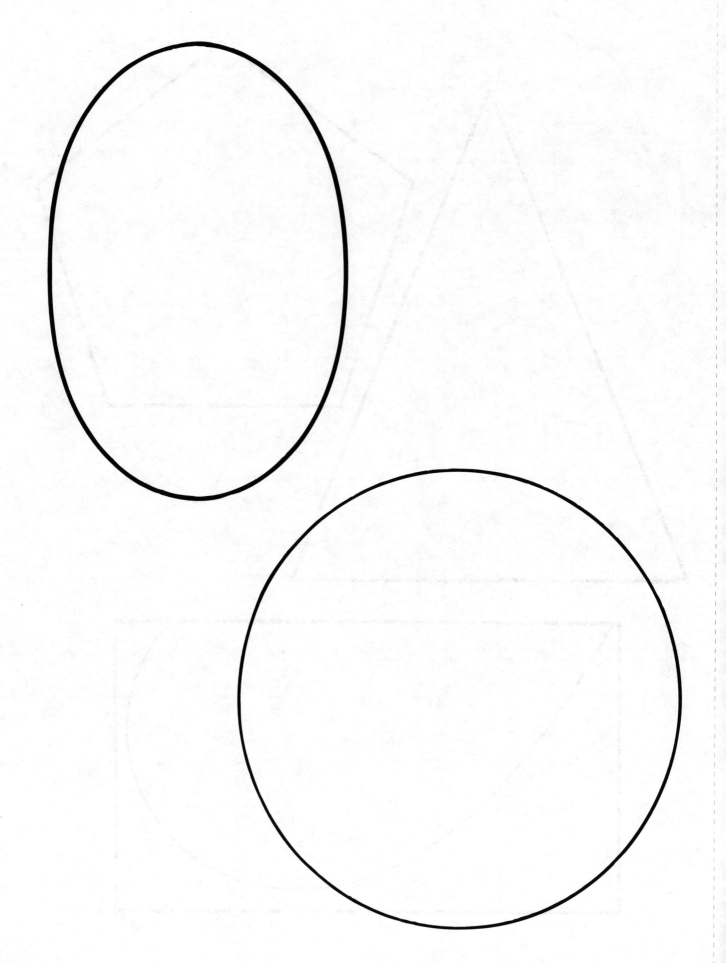

116

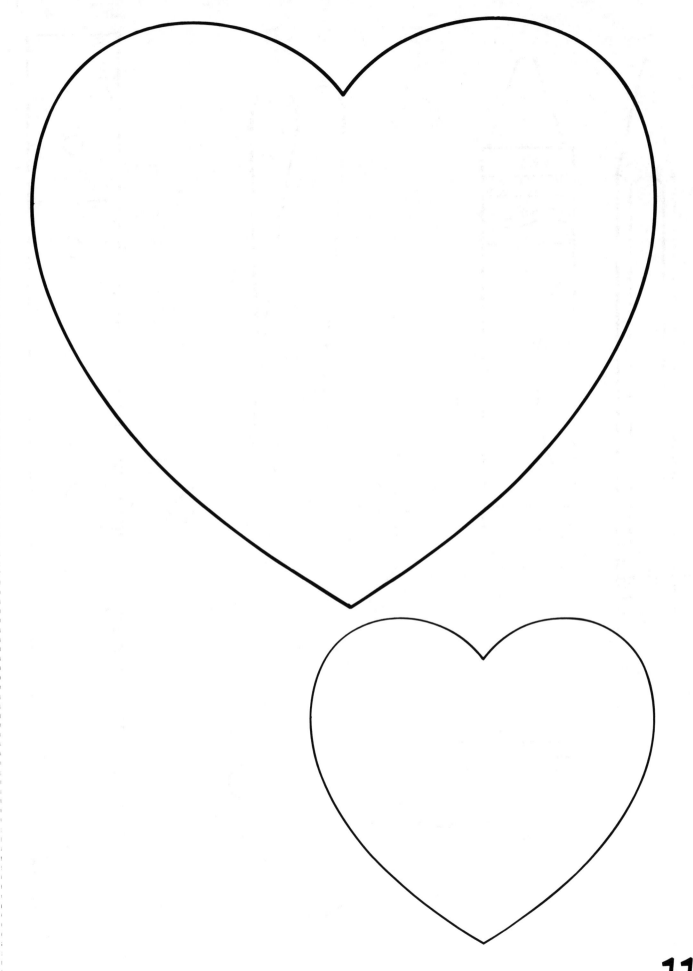

117

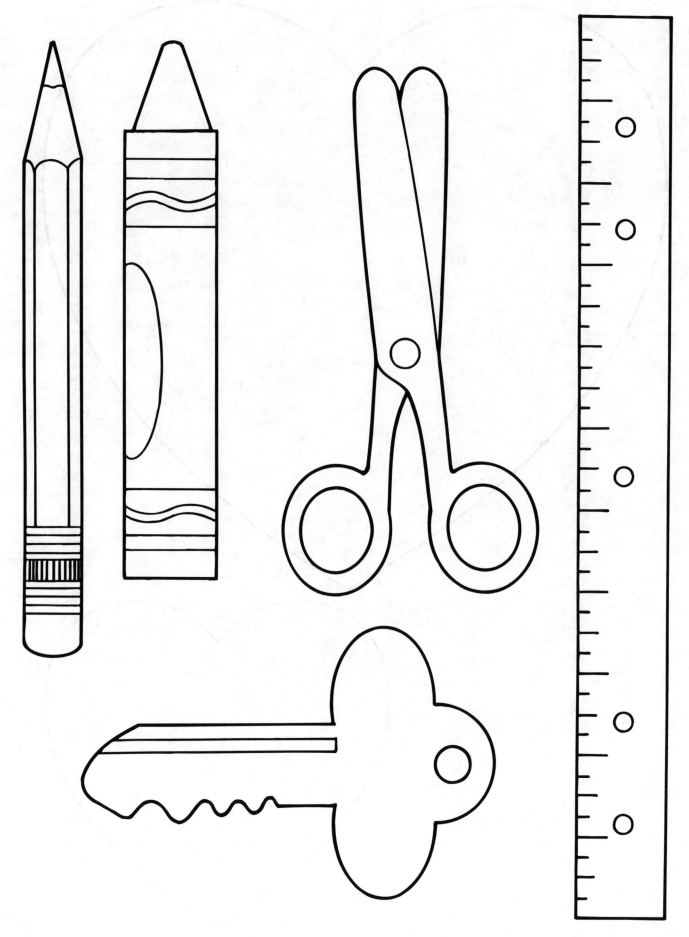

11a

119

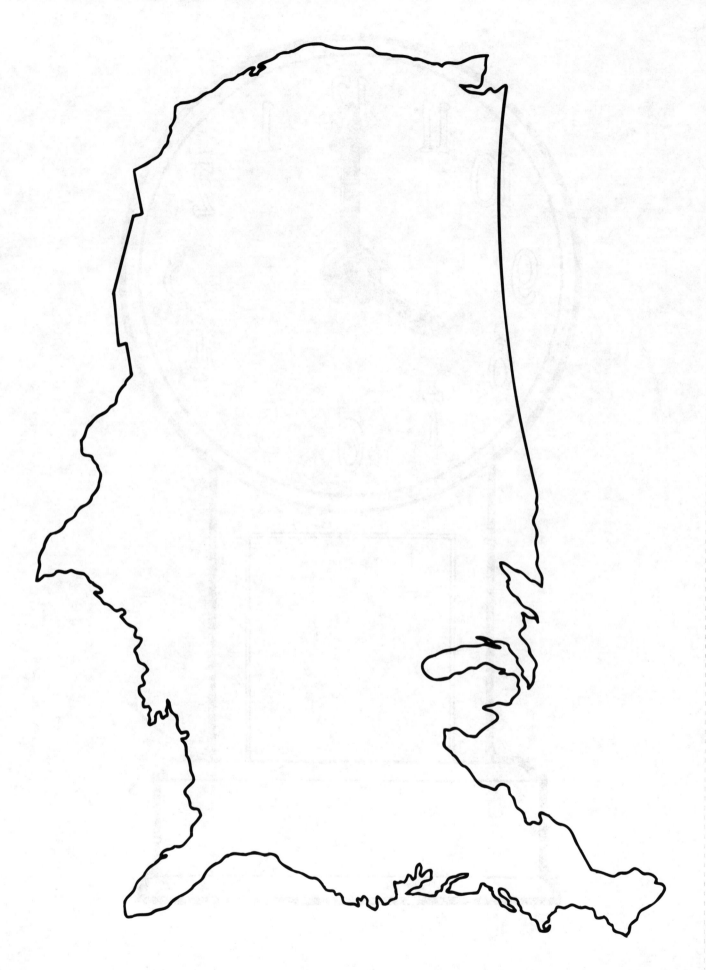

120

121

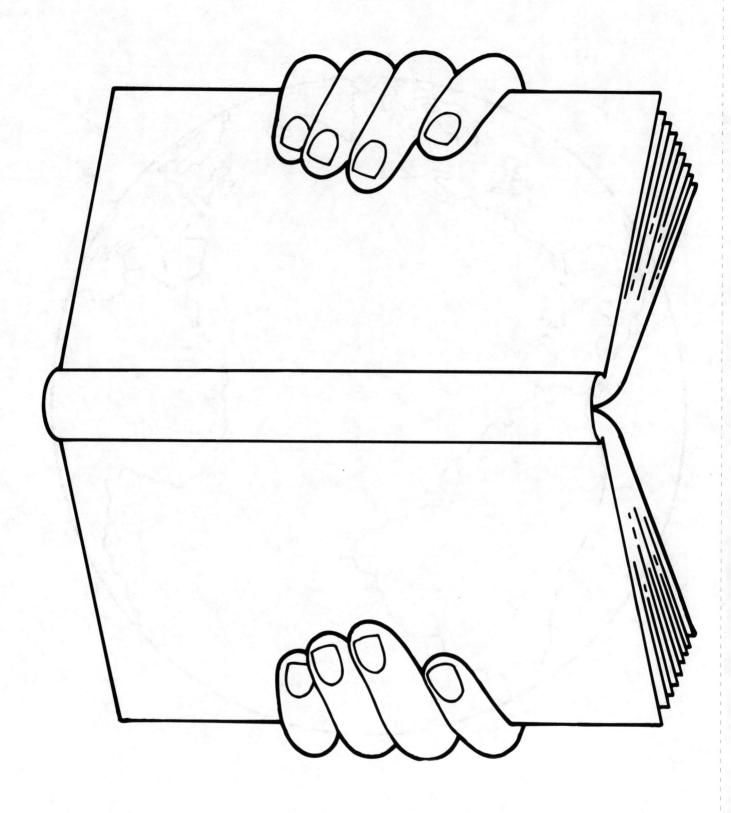

122

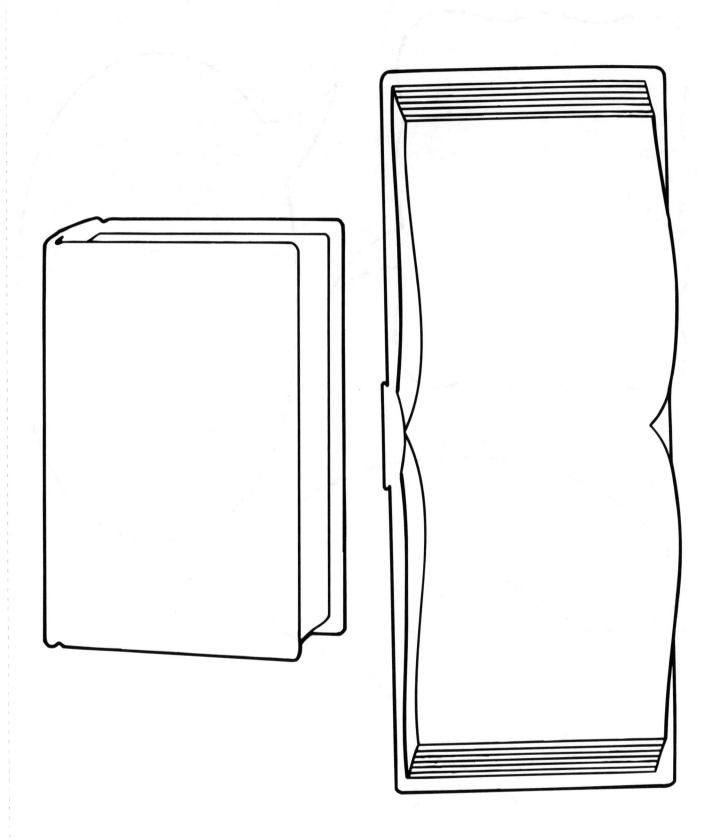

123

124

125

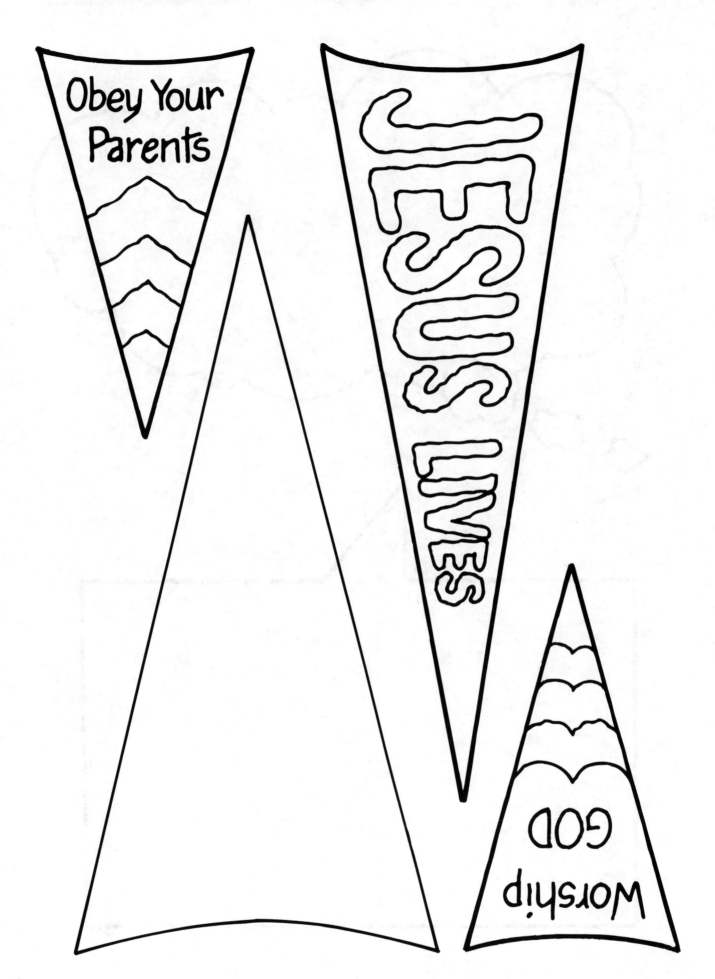

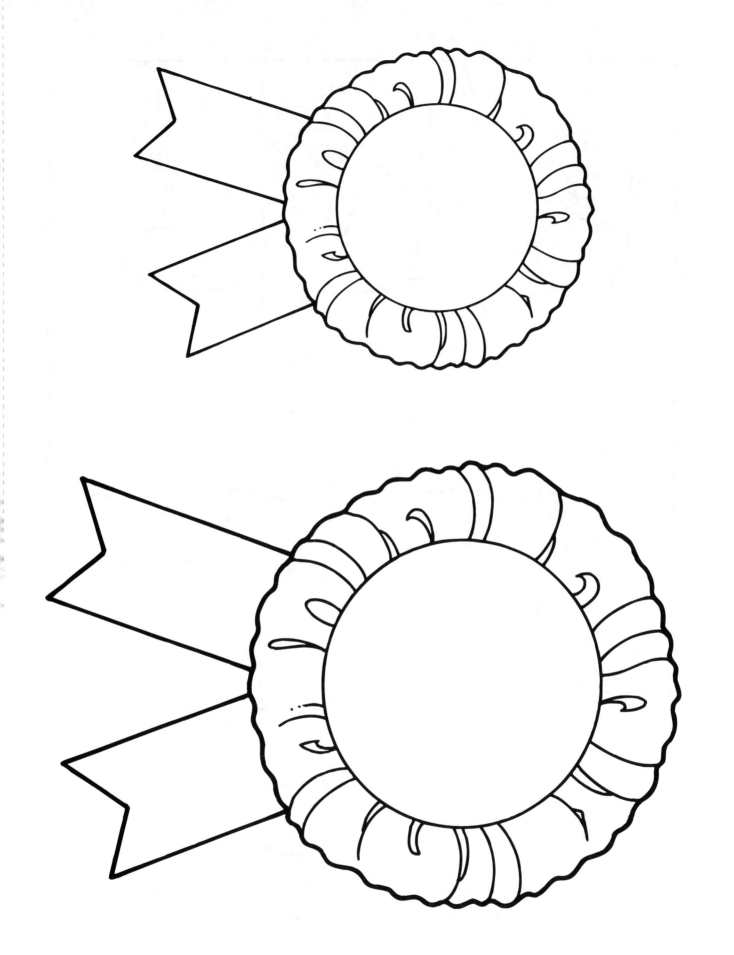

127

128

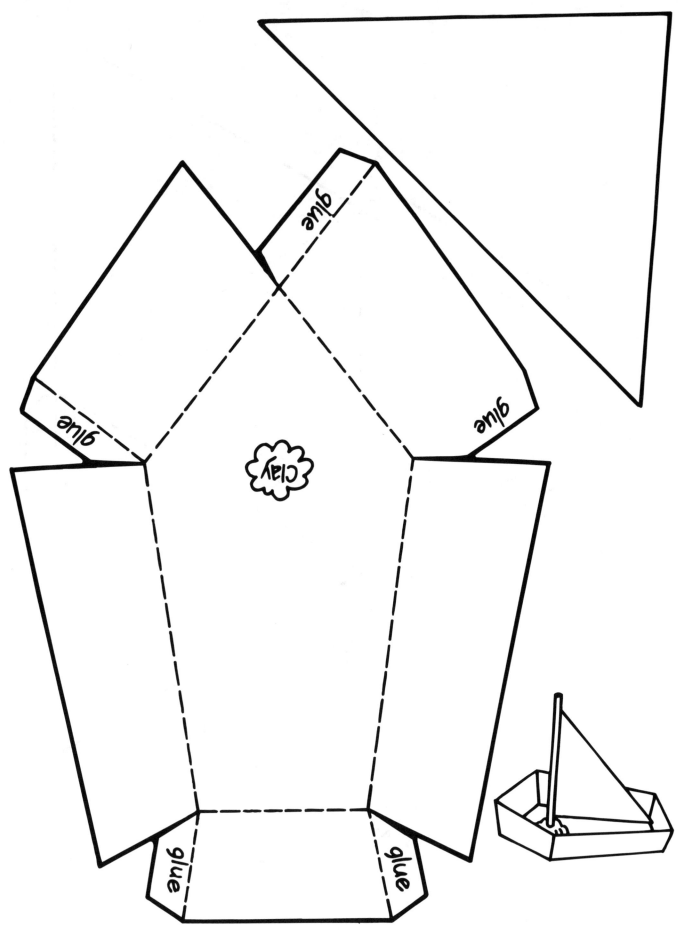

glue

glue

clay

glue

glue

glue

129

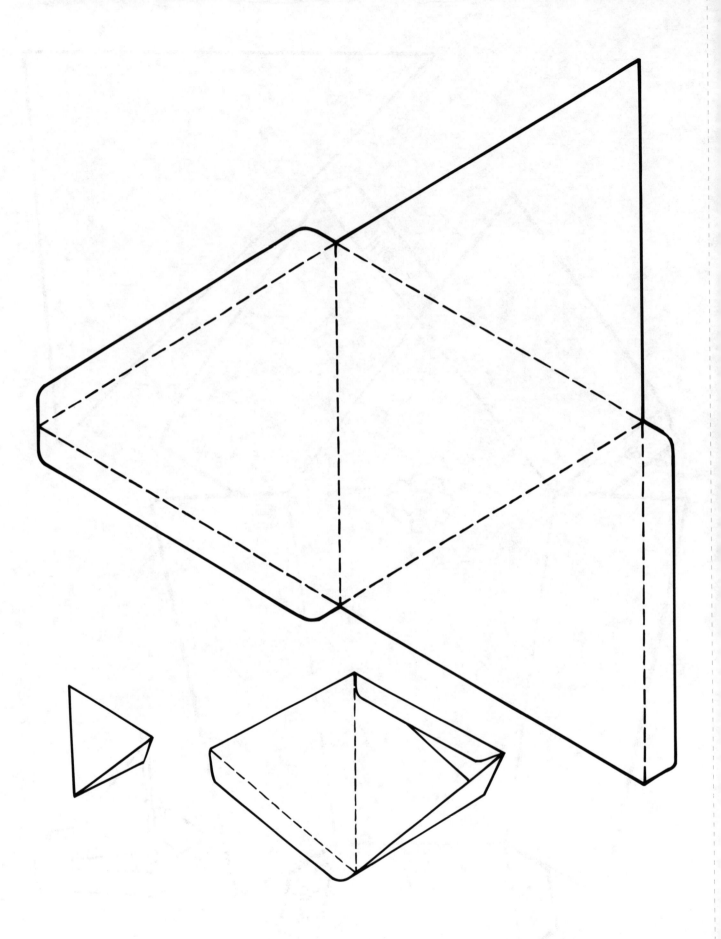

130

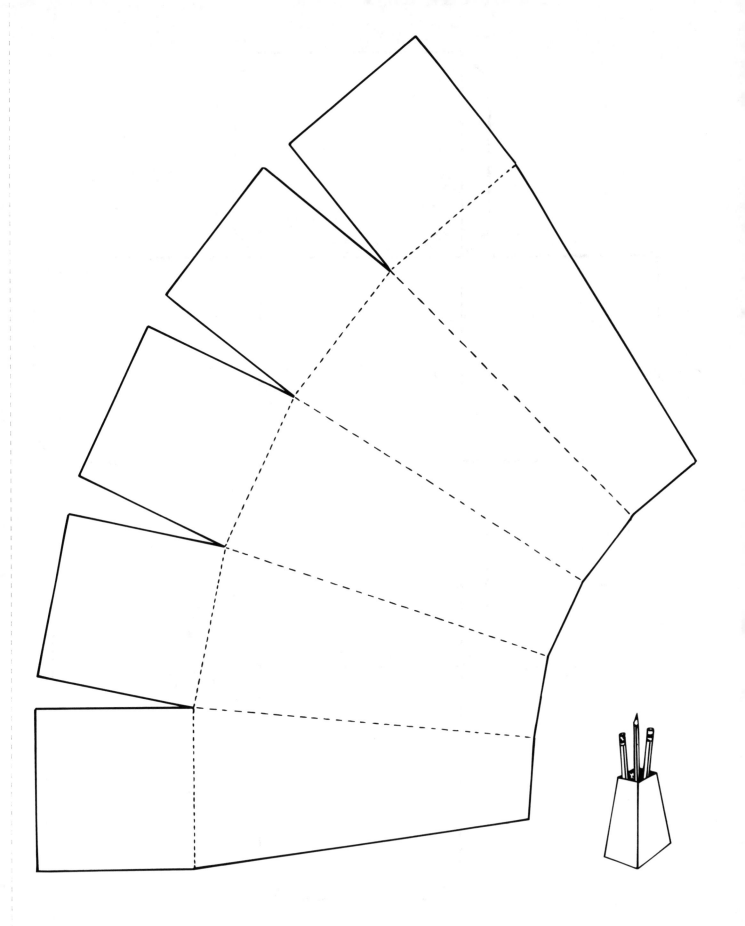

131

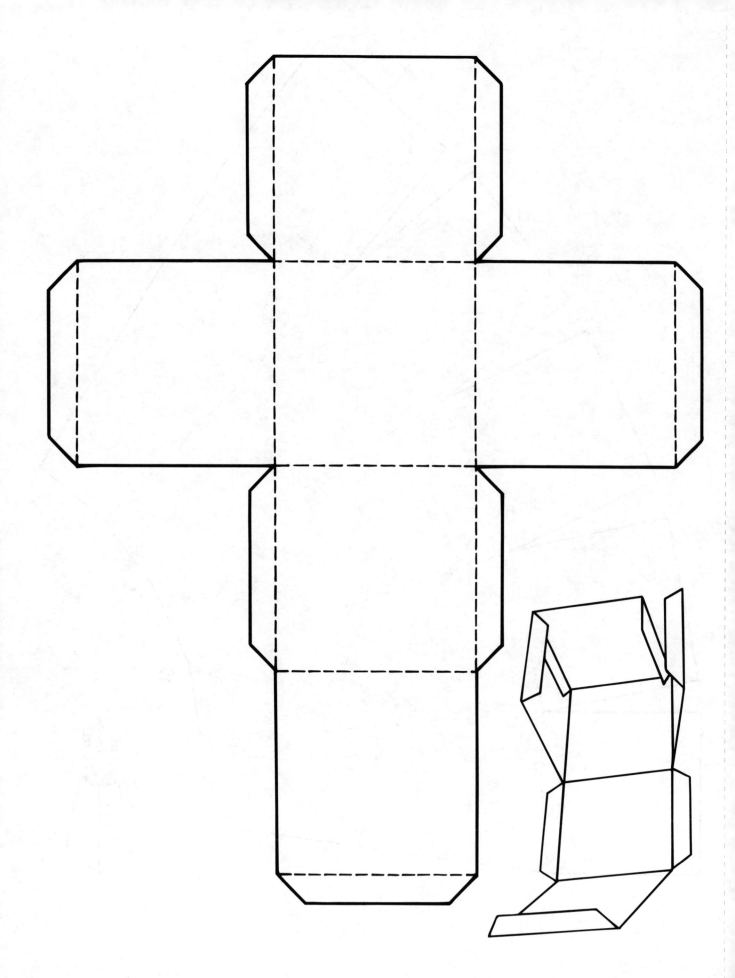

132

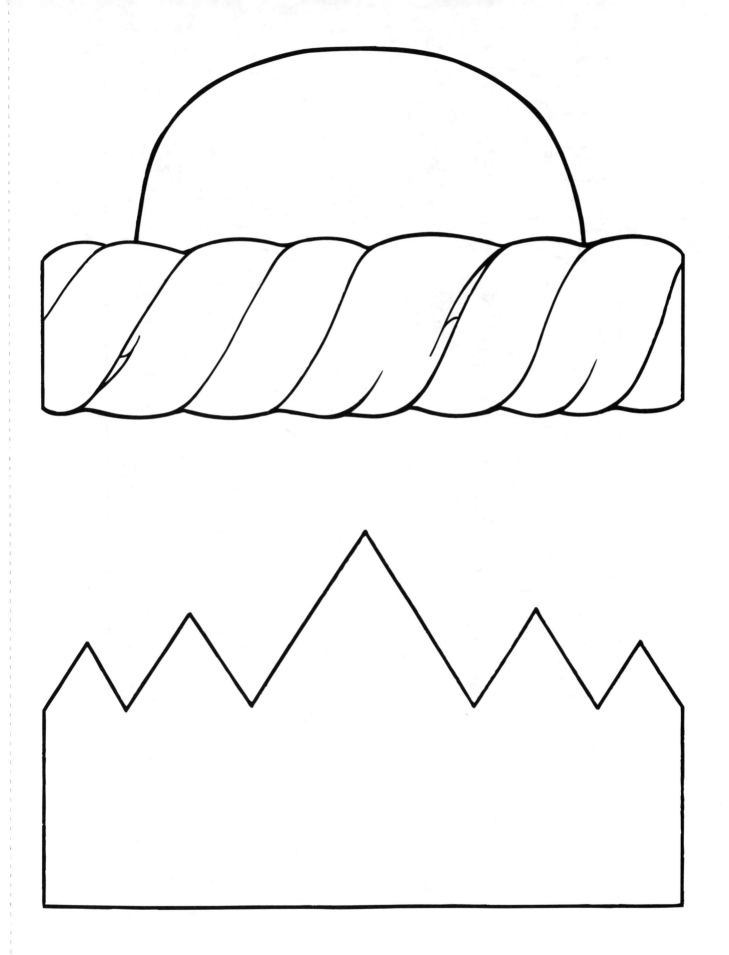

133

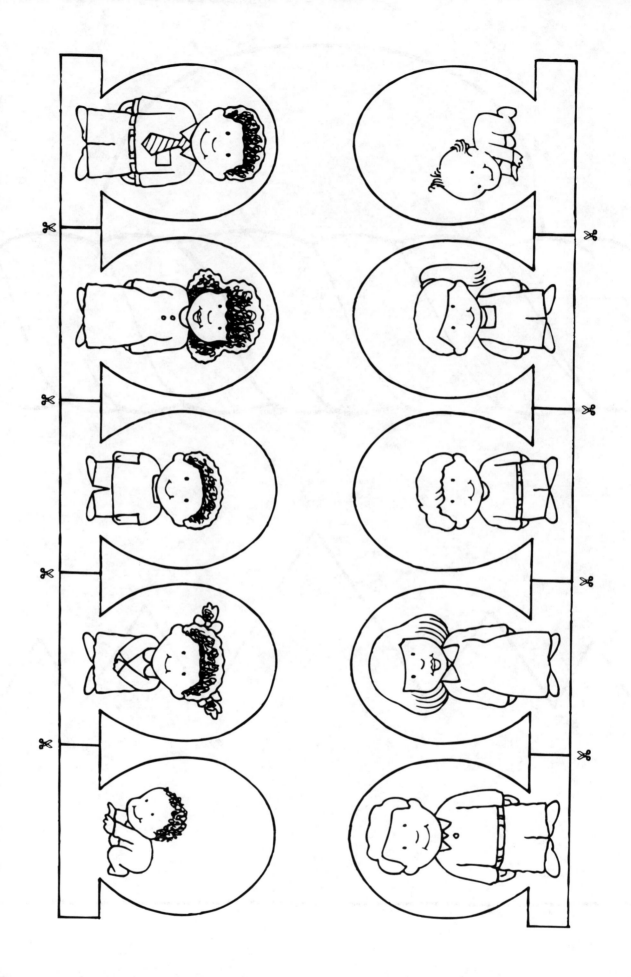

134

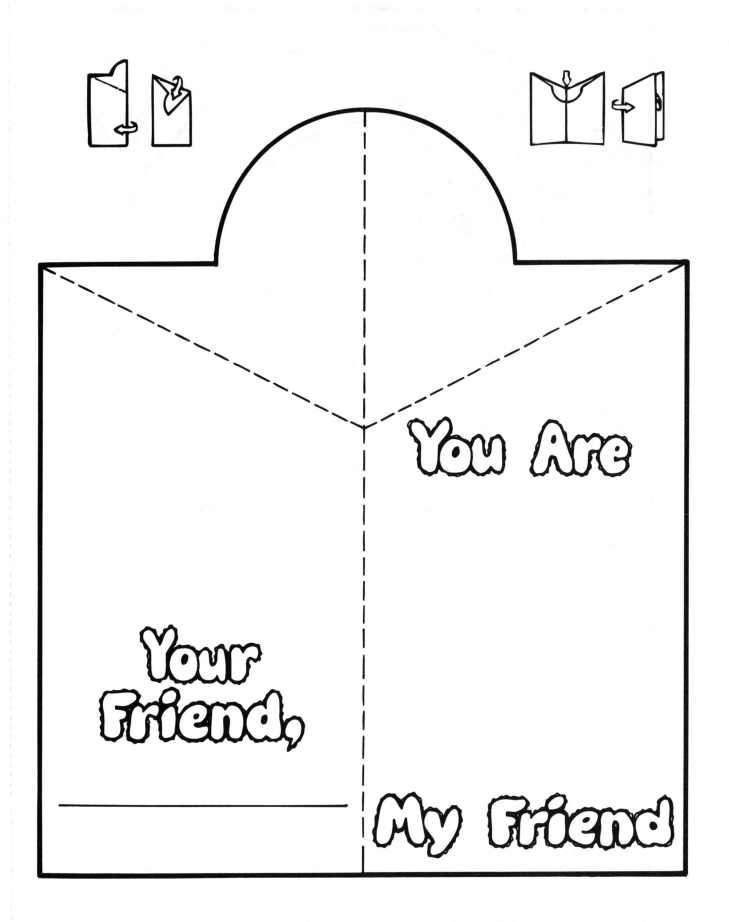

You Are

Your
Friend,

My Friend

135

fold

136

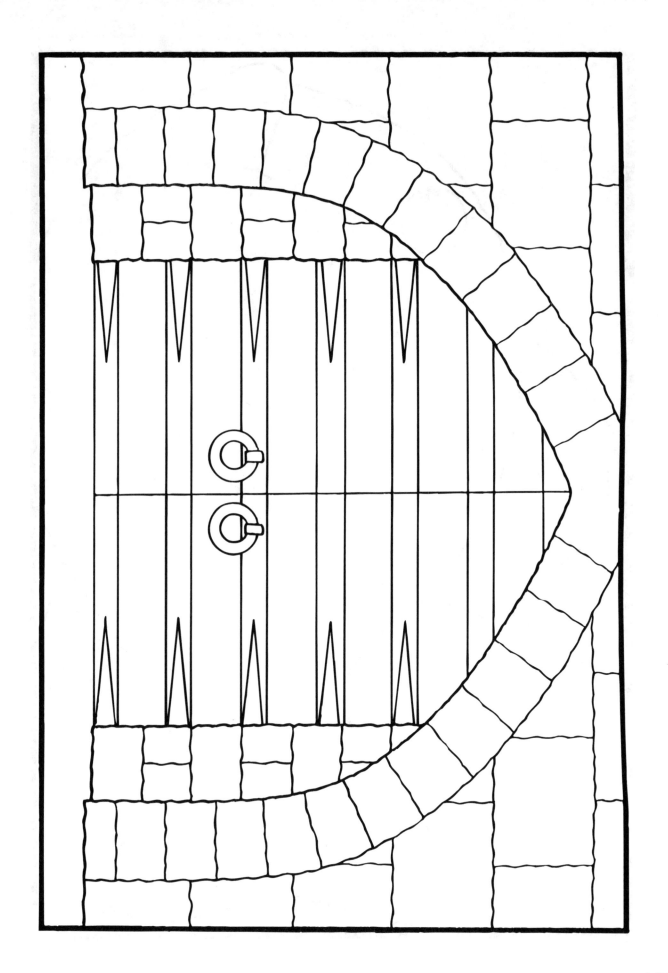

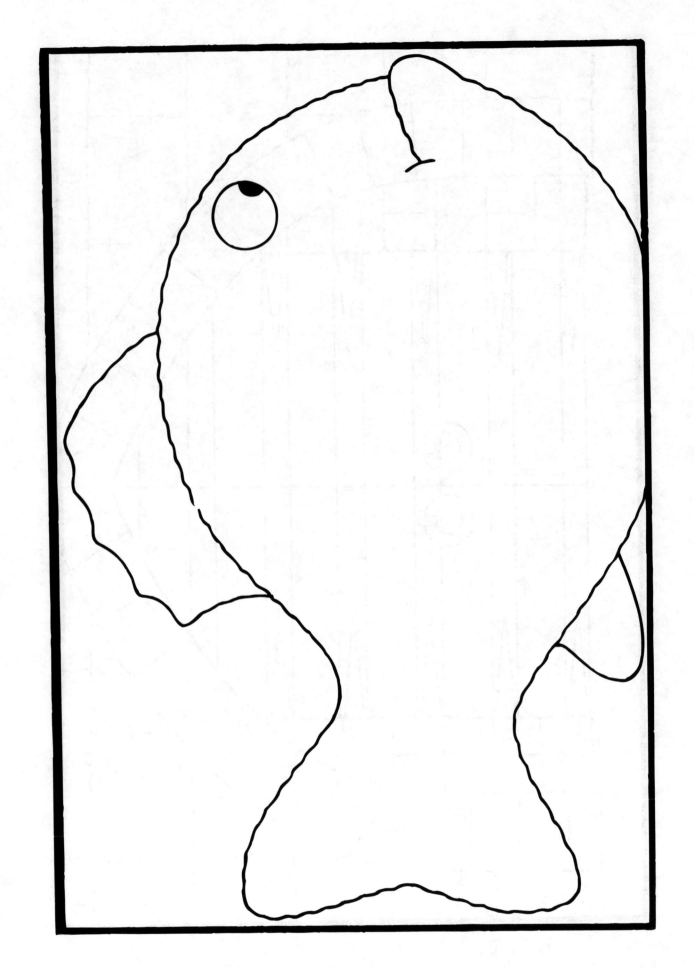

138

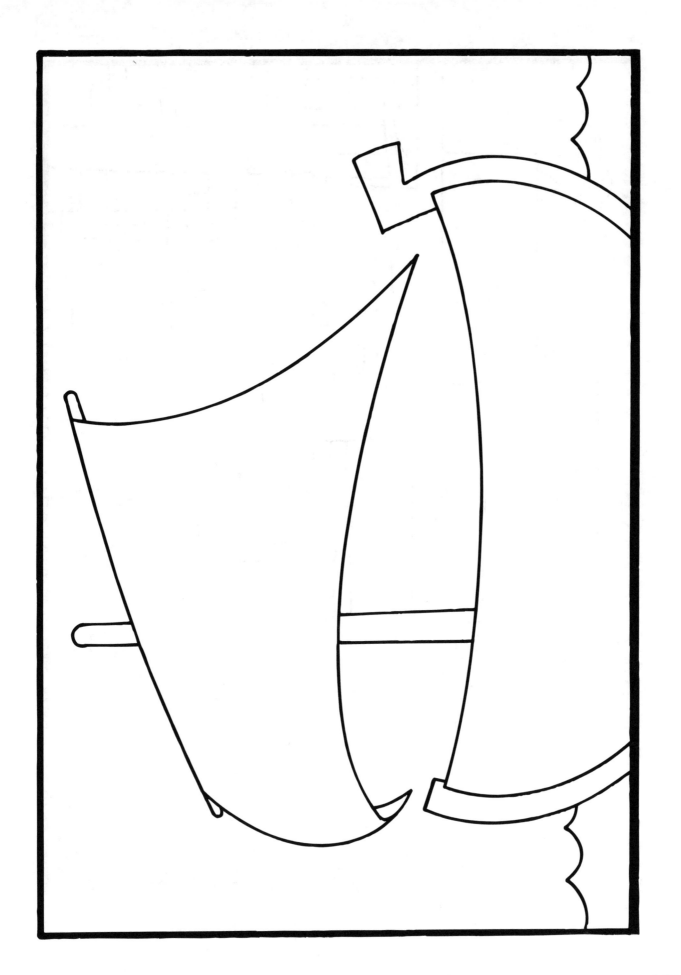

139

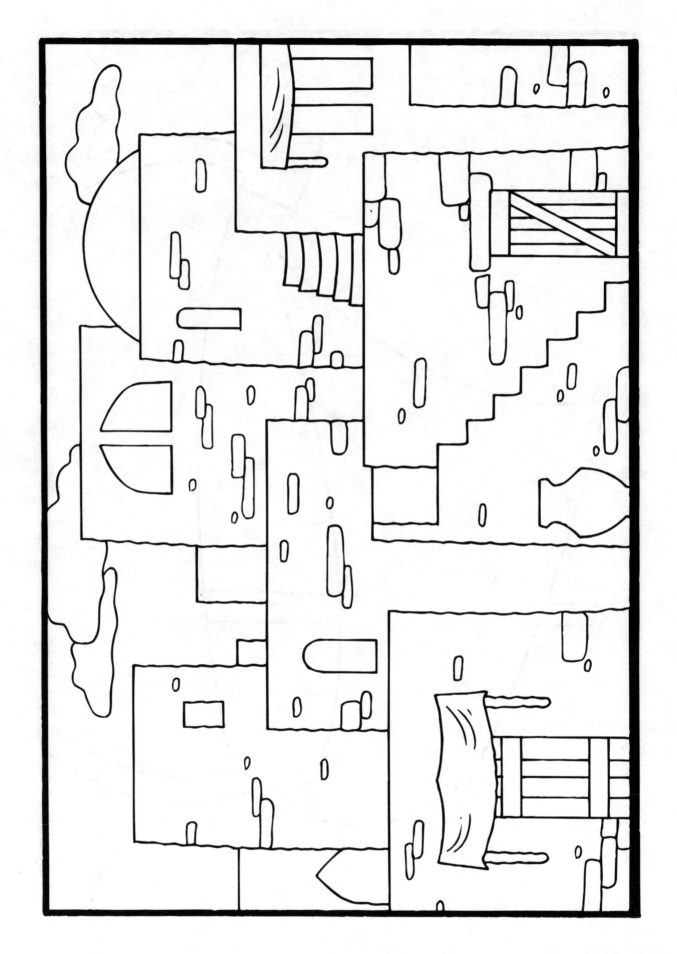

140

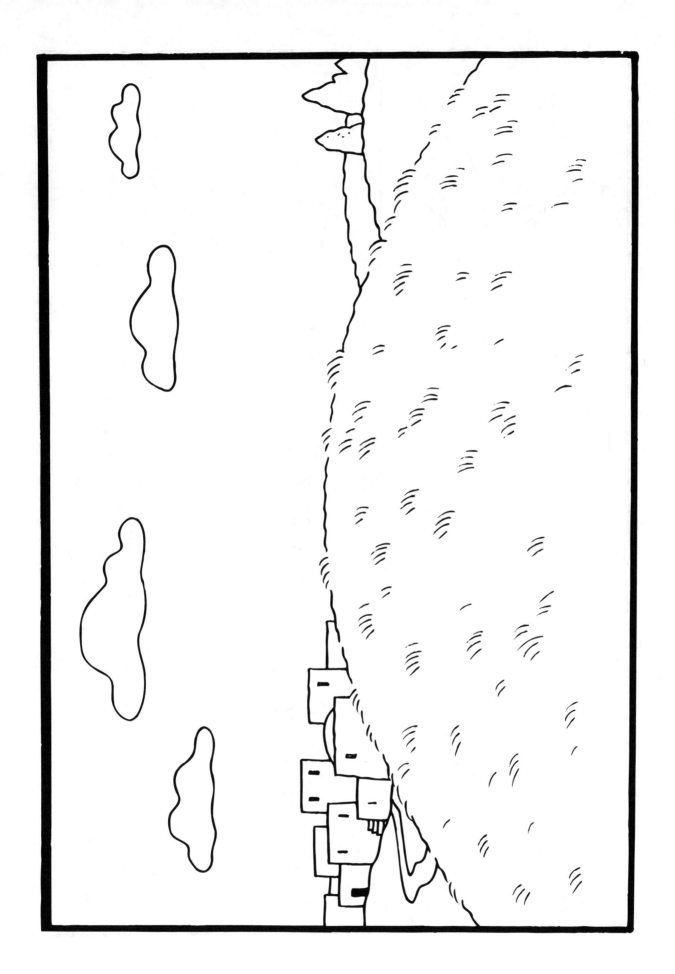

141

142

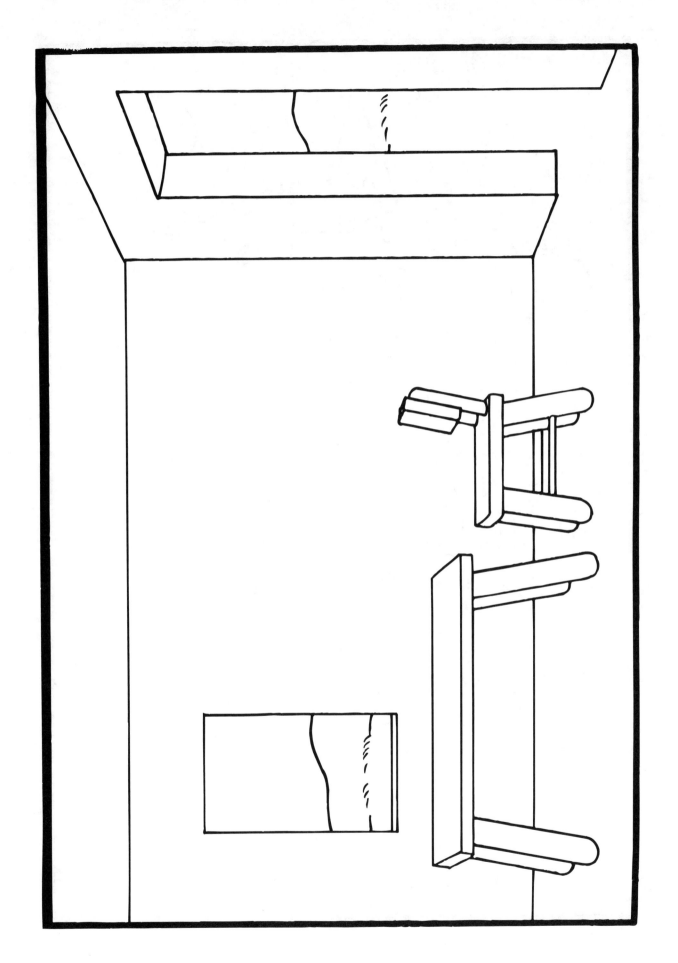

143

144

145

146

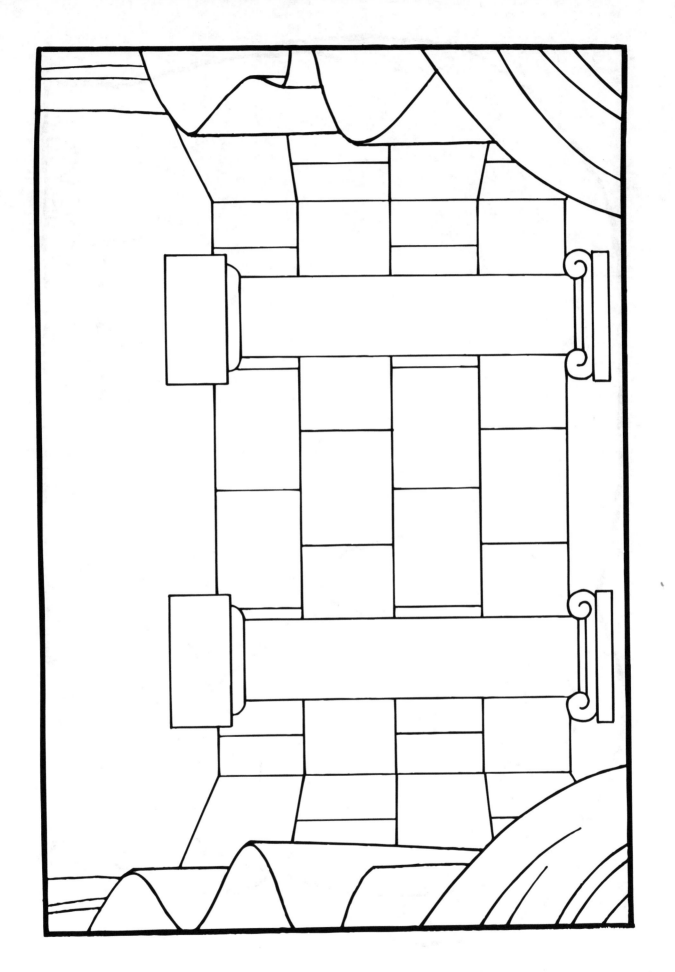

147

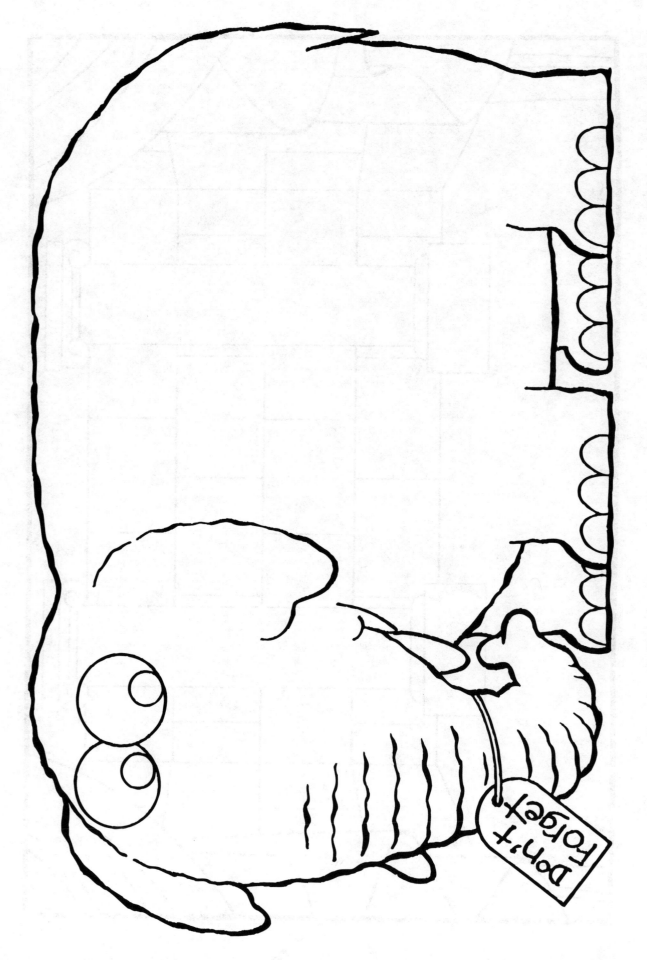

148

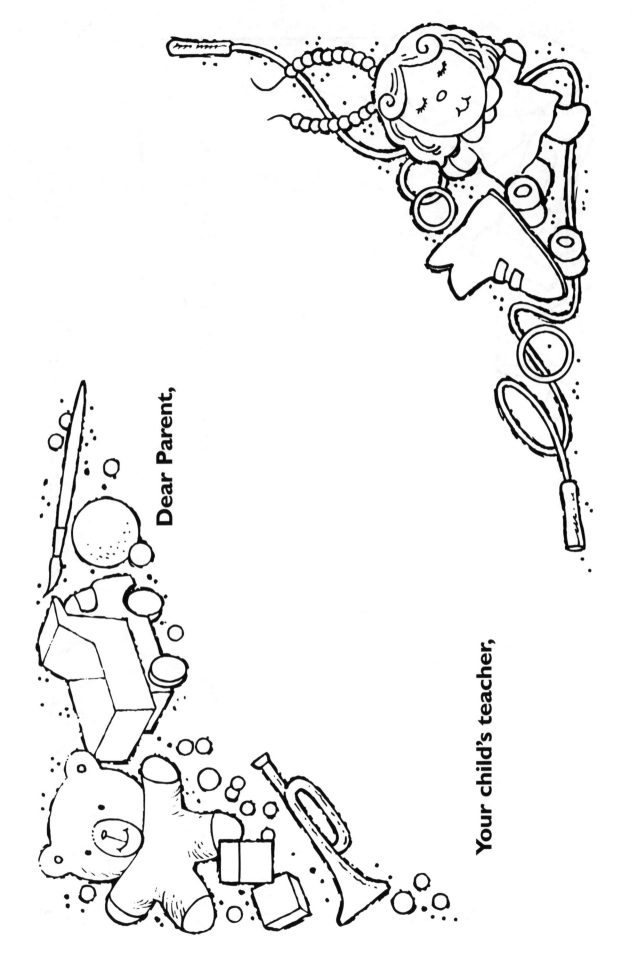

Dear Parent,

Your child's teacher,

149

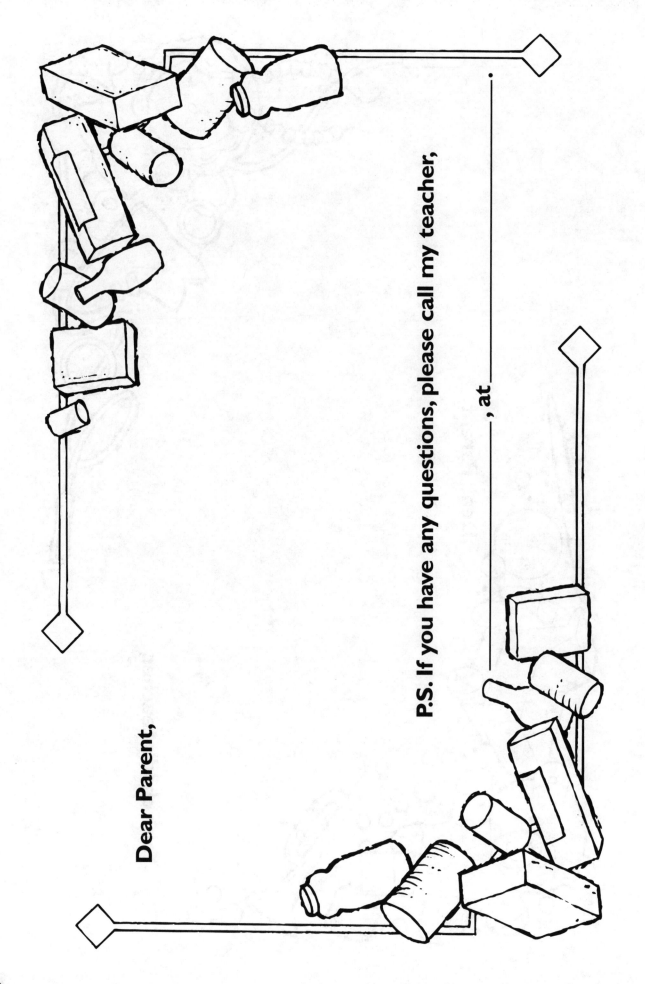

Dear Parent,

P.S. If you have any questions, please call my teacher,

_____ , at

150

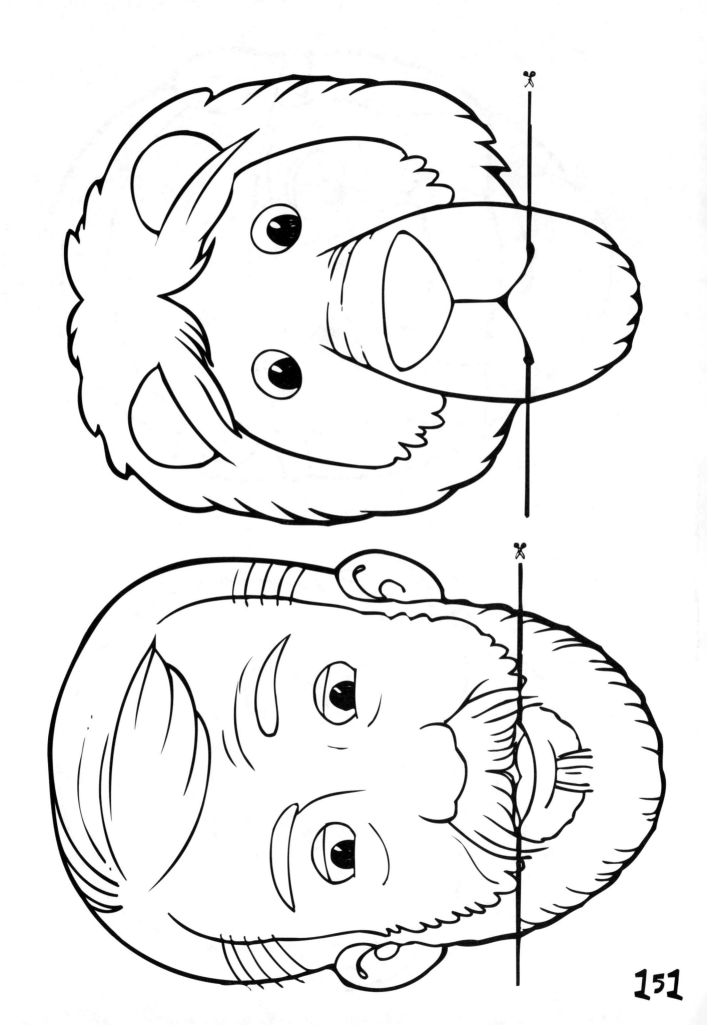

151

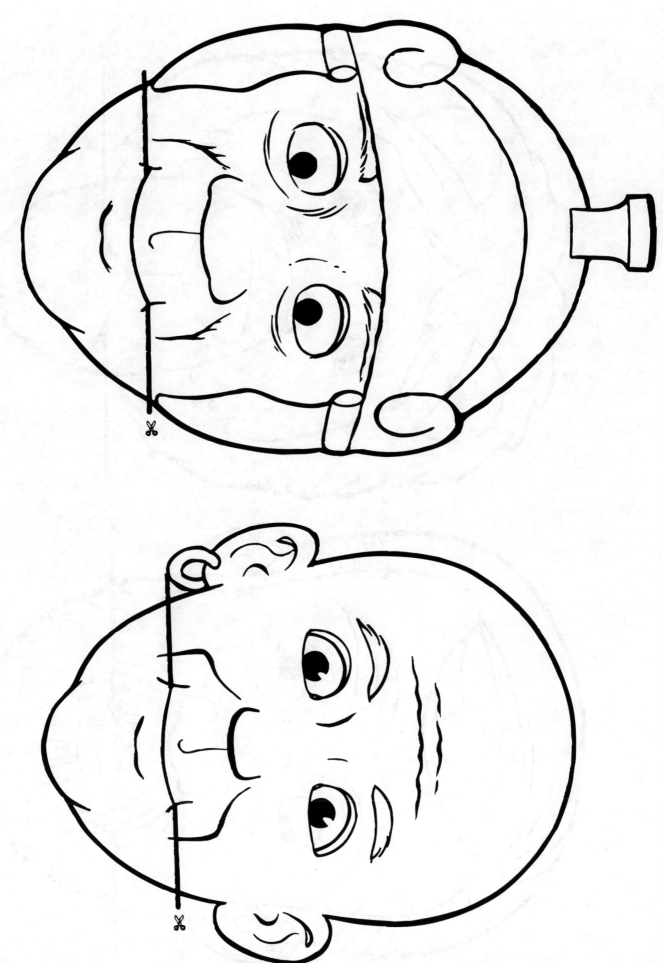

152

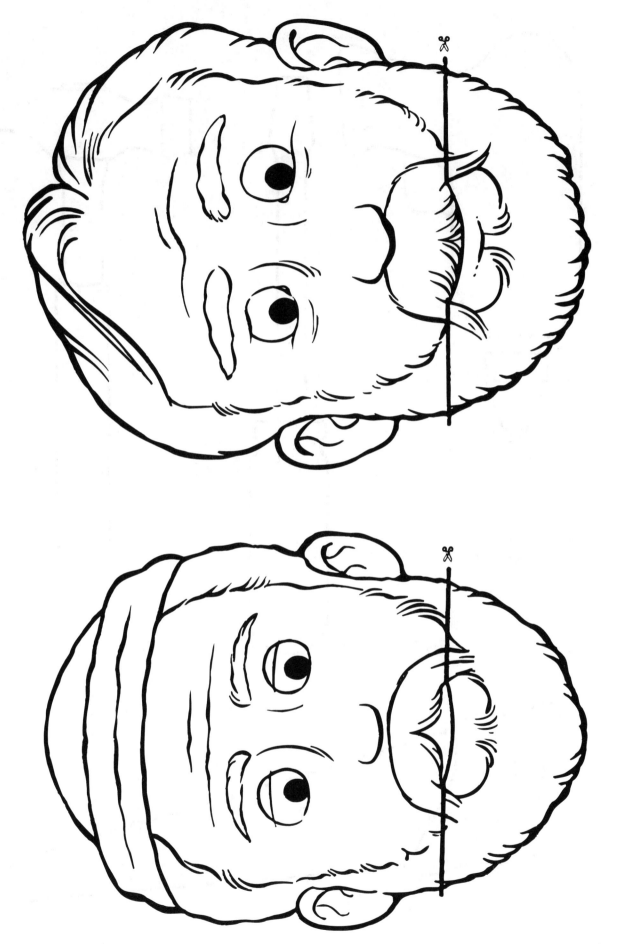

153

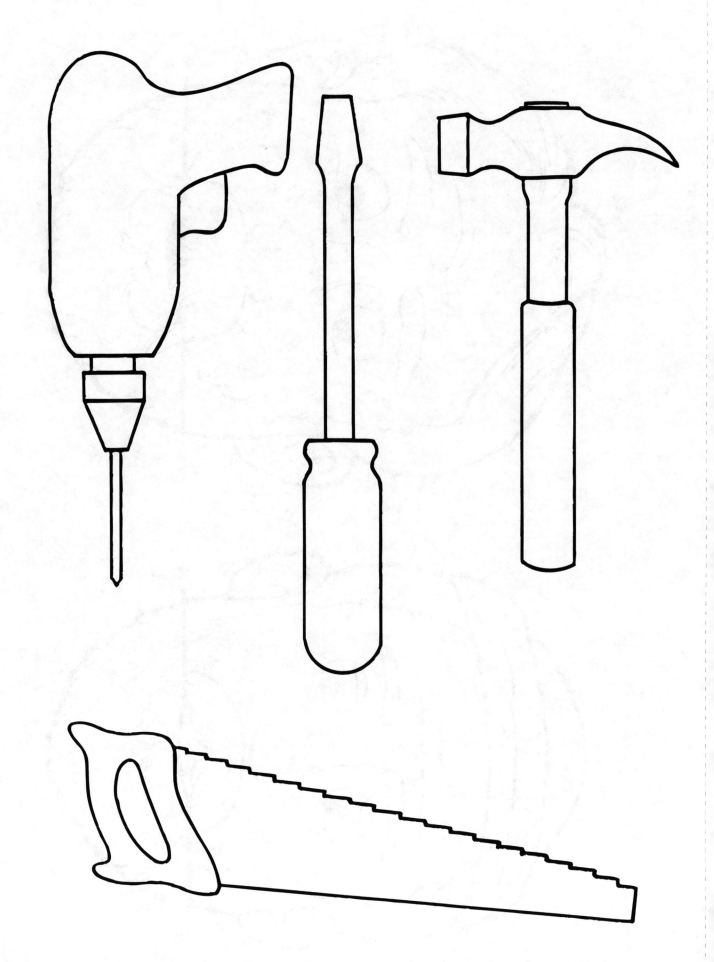

154

155

156

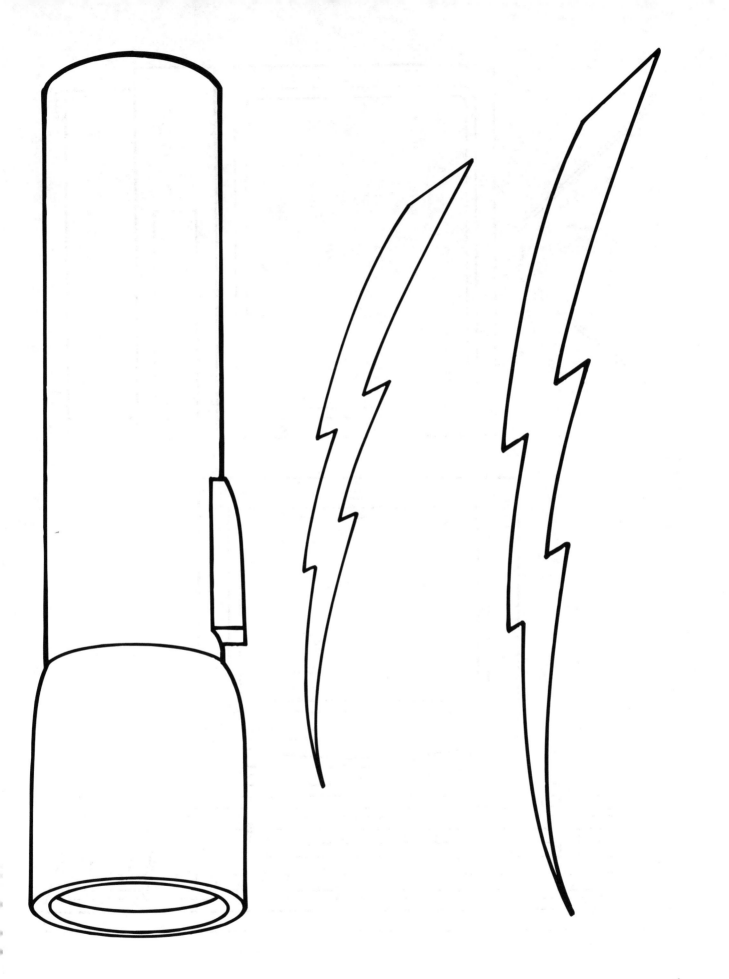

157

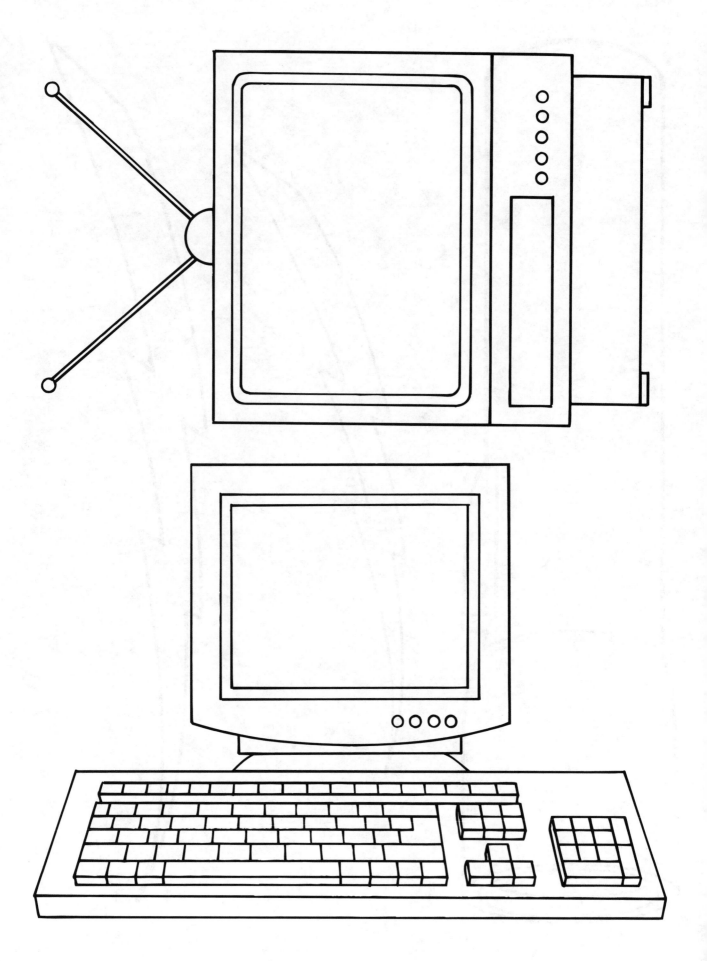

158

Pattern Index

Pattern Index